Gut Health for Women

CRAFTED BY SKRIUWER

Copyright © 2024 by Skriuwer.

All rights reserved. No part of this book may be used or reproduced in any form whatsoever without written permission except in the case of brief quotations in critical articles or reviews.

For more information, contact : **kontakt@skriuwer.com** (www.skriuwer.com)

TABLE OF CONTENTS

CHAPTER 1: INTRODUCTION TO WOMEN'S GUT HEALTH

- *Explains the importance of gut health for women and how the stomach affects mood and overall wellbeing.*
- *Highlights unique female hormonal factors and why women may experience different digestive issues than men.*
- *Provides a brief roadmap of the topics covered in the book.*

CHAPTER 2: THE MICROBES IN OUR BODY

- *Describes the types of bacteria and other tiny organisms living in the gut.*
- *Shows how these microbes help break down food and maintain a balanced digestive system.*
- *Discusses factors that can disrupt this microbial balance.*

CHAPTER 3: HORMONES AND DIGESTION

- *Explores how estrogen, progesterone, and other hormones affect gut movement.*
- *Examines menstrual cycle changes and how they may alter bowel habits.*
- *Suggests dietary tips for better hormone balance and smoother digestion.*

CHAPTER 4: STRESS AND THE DIGESTIVE SYSTEM

- *Reveals the connection between stress hormones and gut function.*
- *Describes common stress-related gut problems, like IBS and reflux.*
- *Offers techniques to reduce stress for better bowel regularity and comfort.*

CHAPTER 5: COMMON DIGESTIVE CONCERNS IN WOMEN

- *Covers topics like IBS, constipation, bloating, diarrhea, and acid reflux.*
- *Talks about specific triggers and tips to cope.*
- *Highlights when it is time to seek professional help.*

CHAPTER 6: THE BRAIN-GUT CONNECTION

- *Explains how signals travel between the stomach and the brain.*
- *Demonstrates how mood can shift when the gut is off balance.*
- *Looks at ways to keep this communication steady for emotional wellbeing.*

CHAPTER 7: NUTRIENTS FOR A HEALTHY GUT

- *Discusses proteins, carbs, fats, vitamins, and minerals essential for digestion.*
- *Shows how nutrient gaps can hurt the gut and overall vitality.*
- *Gives examples of gut-supportive foods.*

CHAPTER 8: PREBIOTICS AND PROBIOTICS

- *Clarifies the difference between feeding existing good bacteria (prebiotics) and adding new ones (probiotics).*
- *Lists food sources and supplements that nourish beneficial microbes.*
- *Suggests practical ways to include both in the daily diet.*

CHAPTER 9: FIBER AND HELPFUL BACTERIA

- *Explains soluble and insoluble fibers and how they help bowel movements.*
- *Shows how fiber feeds the good bacteria and why variety matters.*
- *Advises on controlling gas or bloating when increasing fiber intake.*

CHAPTER 10: REST AND ROUTINE

- *Explores how sleep and daily schedules shape gut function.*
- *Emphasizes consistent bedtime, meal timings, and stress breaks.*
- *Offers tips to balance busy lifestyles with enough rest.*

CHAPTER 11: FOOD SENSITIVITIES

- *Discusses lactose intolerance, gluten sensitivity, FODMAP issues, and more.*
- *Gives testing options and elimination strategies.*
- *Shows how to manage triggers without losing essential nutrients.*

CHAPTER 12: CHANGES OVER THE YEARS

- Walks through puberty, pregnancy, perimenopause, menopause, and beyond.
- Describes how hormone shifts can alter digestion and gut bacteria.
- Gives advice for each stage of a woman's life.

CHAPTER 13: HOW THE GUT AFFECTS MOOD

- Highlights the link between gut chemicals and emotional balance.
- Explains how serotonin, dopamine, and inflammation influence feelings.
- Suggests foods and habits that stabilize gut-driven mood swings.

CHAPTER 14: PHYSICAL ACTIVITY AND DIGESTION

- Shows how gentle movement aids bowel flow and microbial diversity.
- Describes best exercises for women with sensitive stomachs.
- Provides practical tips on timing workouts around meals.

CHAPTER 15: TOXINS AND GUT HEALTH

- Details everyday chemical exposures from food, water, and household products.
- Demonstrates how toxins can upset gut bacteria and hormone balance.
- Gives suggestions for lowering exposure and supporting natural detox.

CHAPTER 16: WOMEN'S HEALTH ISSUES LINKED TO DIGESTION

- Explores endometriosis, PCOS, autoimmune concerns, and how they connect to the gut.
- Addresses UTIs, menstrual irregularities, and fertility with a gut-health lens.
- Shows how stable digestion can ease many female-specific conditions.

CHAPTER 17: HERBS & SUPPLEMENTS FOR SUPPORT

- Reviews popular herbs like ginger, peppermint, and chamomile for gut relief.
- Covers probiotics, fiber supplements, and vitamins that fill nutritional gaps.
- Warns about interactions, quality checks, and proper use.

CHAPTER 18: BUILDING GOOD DAILY HABITS

- *Stresses consistent meal times, balanced nutrition, and simple movement.*
- *Discusses how to organize meal prep and keep stress in check.*
- *Gives guidelines for sustaining routines through changing schedules.*

CHAPTER 19: LONG-TERM CARE FOR THE DIGESTIVE SYSTEM

- *Focuses on adapting to life stages and preventing future gut problems.*
- *Discusses regular check-ups, adjusting diet over time, and handling setbacks.*
- *Encourages flexibility and awareness for lasting digestive health.*

CHAPTER 20: EXAMPLES AND STORIES

- *Shares real-life style stories of women overcoming digestive hurdles.*
- *Illustrates how they tackled IBS, reflux, stress, and food sensitivities.*
- *Offers inspiration for practical solutions and ongoing improvement.*

Chapter 1

Introduction to Women's Gut Health

Gut health is important for everyone, but women often have different needs than men. The stomach and intestines play a key role in breaking down food, taking in nutrients, and keeping out harmful things. Our digestive system also talks with our brain, giving signals about stress, hunger, fullness, and even emotions. When something is off, it can lead to problems such as stomach upset, constipation, or even a change in mood.

Many people might not think much about their gut. They may only pay attention when they get a stomachache or feel bloated. But the health of the stomach and intestines is important for many reasons. This includes the way you feel from day to day, your emotional balance, and your body's ability to handle stress. In women, these issues are especially important because of hormone fluctuations that happen at different times.

1.1 Why Women's Gut Health Is Unique

Women's bodies go through many changes from puberty to menopause. These changes involve hormones like estrogen and progesterone. They can affect digestion and the balance of microbes that live in the intestines. For example, some women may notice they have more stomach pain or bloating before a menstrual cycle. Others may find that their digestion changes after childbirth or as they get older.

Women are also more likely than men to experience certain digestive problems, like irritable bowel syndrome (IBS). Part of this might be because of the way hormones affect the gut. Another reason is that women can have different stress responses than men. Stress can change the way the gut works, possibly leading to more frequent bowel movements or constipation.

1.2 The Role of Gut Bacteria

Inside the digestive tract are trillions of tiny microbes. These include bacteria, fungi, viruses, and more. Many of these are helpful. Some are less helpful, but they are kept in check by the good microbes. When the helpful ones are plentiful, they support digestion by breaking down food, making vitamins, and protecting the gut lining. They also help control harmful bacteria.

Women's gut bacteria can shift for many reasons. Hormonal changes, stress, diet, antibiotics, or even traveling to a new place can change the balance. When the balance of good and less helpful bacteria shifts too much, a woman may experience problems like gas, bloating, diarrhea, or other signs of upset. Keeping these microbes happy is a big part of staying healthy.

1.3 Connection to Mental Wellbeing

The gut and brain work closely together. They use nerve signals, hormones, and chemical messengers to communicate. If the stomach is upset, the brain can sense it. This can lead to feelings of worry or sadness. On the other hand, if someone is very worried or tense, the gut may feel it, which can cause pain or changes in bowel habits.

Women often carry many responsibilities, like work, caregiving, and running a household. Stress from these tasks can affect the gut. Over time, chronic stress might reduce the good microbes and allow the less helpful ones to grow. This can start a cycle of gut trouble that leads to even more tension.

1.4 Early Warnings of Digestive Problems

It is helpful to know the signs that show your gut may be struggling. These might include:

- Frequent bloating or gas
- Changes in bowel habits (constipation or diarrhea)
- Stomach pain or cramping
- Feeling tired all the time
- Unexpected changes in weight
- Skin issues like acne or rashes
- Mood swings or increased worry
- Brain fog or having a hard time focusing

While these signs can happen to men too, women may notice them more often because of hormone shifts and other factors. Paying attention can help you catch issues early and keep them from getting worse.

1.5 Why This Book Matters

Some books talk about gut health in a general way. Others focus on women's health but do not address the gut specifically. This book tries to bring both views together. It takes into account the unique factors that affect women's digestive systems, while also offering a deeper look at the brain-gut link.

Throughout the chapters, we will explore things like:

- Which nutrients help keep the gut strong
- How stress affects women's digestion
- Ways to support good bacteria through fiber, prebiotics, and probiotics
- How to deal with common digestive problems without repeating the same old tips
- The impact of toxins in everyday life
- How to build healthy habits that last
- Real stories that highlight different ways women handle gut issues

By following the ideas in the book, women can strengthen their digestive systems, support mental wellbeing, and reduce the problems caused by an off-balance gut.

1.6 How to Use This Book

This book is meant to be read from start to finish, so each chapter builds on the one before it. But if you already have knowledge in some areas, you can jump to the chapters that interest you the most. Try to keep an open mind. Even if a concept sounds advanced, it will be explained in clear terms. Remember that each person's body is unique. What works for one person may not be best for another.

It might help to keep a simple journal while reading. If you notice that certain foods or habits make you feel better or worse, write them down. This will help you track your progress and learn what works for your body.

1.7 The Bigger Picture

Gut health is just one part of overall wellbeing. For women, staying aware of how hormones, stress, and lifestyle choices affect digestion is key. Over time, small changes can add up to big improvements. This might involve choosing foods that feed the good bacteria, finding ways to deal with stress, and getting enough sleep. It might also mean looking at how different stages of life affect your stomach.

In the chapters ahead, we will discuss many topics. We will go through hormones, microbial balance, stress, foods, and more. The goal is to give you clear information you can use right away. These lessons may help with digestive comfort, mental clarity, and long-term health.

1.8 Stepping into a Deeper Understanding

We want you to have a full picture of how your stomach and mind affect each other. When your gut is in a good state, you may have more energy, better mood balance, and fewer physical troubles. When it is off-balance, it can be hard to feel good, no matter what else you do.

Many factors can affect the gut, so we must look at more than just food. Stress, relationships, and even your daily schedule can all play roles. We also need to think about potential toxins in the environment or household products that might affect the gut.

Before we start learning about the smaller details, it helps to keep in mind that you have some control over your gut's health. Small steps in the right direction can have a big impact over time. By having a basic understanding of how the gut works and what can harm it, you will be better prepared to make the best choices for your body.

1.9 Conclusion to Chapter 1

Gut health affects much more than digestion. It can change how we think, feel, and act every day. For women, these issues are often more complicated because of hormone changes, stress levels, and other life factors. However, by learning how to support the gut, it is possible to see improvements in both physical and emotional wellbeing.

In the next chapter, we will look at the microbes in our bodies. This topic is at the heart of gut health. Understanding how these tiny helpers work, what can harm them, and how to keep them balanced will set the stage for all the other areas we will explore in this book.

Chapter 2

The Microbes in Our Body

Many of us have heard that bacteria can cause illness. But not all bacteria are harmful. In fact, our bodies rely on certain kinds of bacteria to function. The gut is home to trillions of these microbes, including bacteria, fungi, viruses, and other organisms. While this can sound alarming, many of them are good. They keep bad bacteria from taking over and help our bodies do tasks we cannot do on our own.

2.1 A Quick Look at Microbes

Microbes are tiny living things that can only be seen with a microscope. They come in many forms. Some are friendly and help with digestion, while others can lead to sickness if they grow too much. In a healthy gut, these various microbes work together in balance. This helps keep the lining of the gut strong, so harmful particles do not slip into the bloodstream.

When we talk about the gut, we usually mean the part of the body that starts at the mouth and ends at the anus. But the biggest concentration of microbes is found in the large intestine, also called the colon. This is where most of the action happens.

2.2 Why Microbes Matter for Women

Men and women share many of the same microbes. However, women's bodies can be affected by changes in these microbes in specific ways. For instance, when certain bacteria grow too much, they might affect how estrogen is broken down. This could lead to changes in mood or more serious conditions. Women also have a different hormone environment, which can affect the pH level and other factors in the body.

Some women may experience gut changes right before a menstrual cycle or around menopause. This could be linked to shifts in bacterial balance. Stress is another factor. Studies show that stress hormones can reduce the number of helpful bacteria in the gut. Women, who often juggle many roles, may experience higher levels of chronic stress, which can change their microbial balance even more.

2.3 How Microbes Help with Digestion

Microbes break down parts of our food that our own enzymes cannot handle. For example, they can help digest certain fibers, turning them into smaller molecules that fuel the cells in our colon. These smaller molecules, such as short-chain fatty acids, help with gut lining health. They may also support immune function and keep inflammation in check.

This is especially important for women because the gut barrier can be stressed by hormone changes. If the gut is weak or inflamed, it can contribute to problems like bloating, discomfort, and, in some cases, immune system issues. By eating foods that feed these microbes properly, you help them do their job in protecting and supporting your body.

2.4 Microbes and Mood

The gut and brain talk to each other through nerve signals, chemical messengers, and even direct pathways through the bloodstream. When gut microbes break down food, they release chemicals that can affect mood and stress responses. Some microbes produce substances that help keep inflammation low, which is linked to fewer mood problems.

For women, who might be more likely to have mood-related concerns around certain times of the month, having a balanced gut can be a key piece in feeling more stable. It can also be an important factor for those dealing with long-term mood struggles or a sense of worry. While there are many causes for these issues, good gut health can be part of a broader plan to feel better.

2.5 Protecting the Gut Wall

One important job of gut microbes is to help keep the lining of the gut intact. The gut wall is only one cell layer thick, so it can be vulnerable. Helpful bacteria encourage the cells of the gut wall to stick together and repair themselves as needed. They also create substances that feed these cells, ensuring they stay healthy.

When the gut wall becomes leaky, substances can enter the bloodstream that are not supposed to be there. This is sometimes called "leaky gut." It can lead to immune responses, which may show up as skin problems, tiredness, joint pain, or mood issues. In women, it might also contribute to hormone-related concerns because the body is under more stress.

2.6 What Can Harm the Microbes

The balance of gut microbes can be disrupted by several things, including:

- Antibiotics: While these medicines kill harmful bacteria, they can also reduce helpful bacteria if used often or for long periods.
- Poor Diet: High intake of processed foods, sugar, and unhealthy fats can reduce the variety of helpful bacteria.
- Stress: Chronic stress can change the gut environment, allowing less helpful microbes to become more common.
- Lack of Sleep: Sleep is important for the body's recovery. Without enough rest, the gut ecosystem can suffer.
- Environmental Toxins: Certain chemicals in the air, food, and water can change the gut environment.
- Hormone Changes: Shifts in hormones can affect the environment in which microbes live, leading to changes in bacterial balance.

2.7 How to Support Good Microbes

The good news is that there are practical ways to help your gut microbes. We will explore these in more detail in later chapters, but here are some key steps to keep in mind:

1. **Varied Diet**: Eating a range of whole foods can help different types of friendly microbes grow.
2. **Fiber Intake**: Fiber is important for feeding good microbes. Whole grains, fruits, vegetables, nuts, and seeds are great sources.
3. **Prebiotics and Probiotics**: Certain foods or supplements can feed existing good microbes or add new ones to your system.
4. **Stress Management**: Keeping stress under control can help maintain a balanced gut.
5. **Limit Antibiotic Use**: Only use antibiotics when truly needed, and consider taking a quality probiotic afterward.

6. **Adequate Sleep**: Aim for good rest each night to allow the body to restore balance.

2.8 Unique Tips for Women

Since women can be more impacted by hormone fluctuations, they can benefit from paying attention to times when hormones change, like before a monthly cycle, after childbirth, or around menopause. Observing how the gut feels during these times can be informative. If you notice consistent problems, simple changes in diet or the use of supplements might help maintain a smoother digestive process.

It is also important to consider how birth control pills or hormone replacement therapy might affect your gut microbes. Some women find that these options lead to a shift in digestion or cause bloating. If this happens, speaking to a health professional about your symptoms could lead to solutions that better match your body's needs.

2.9 Getting Tested

For women who have serious or long-term gut troubles, medical tests can reveal more about what is happening inside the gut. One common test is a stool analysis, which looks at the types of microbes present. This test can also show if there are signs of inflammation or if certain bad microbes are overabundant.

Another type of test checks for food sensitivities. While these are not always perfect, they can give clues about which foods might be causing issues. In some cases, a breath test might be used to check for small intestinal bacterial overgrowth (SIBO), which is when bacteria that belong in the large intestine grow in the small intestine instead, leading to bloating and discomfort.

2.10 The Future of Microbe Research

Scientists are learning more and more about gut microbes each day. New studies show that certain bacteria might help with weight control, mood, and even how well the body handles glucose. This area is evolving fast, and many believe that in the future, we will have personalized treatments based on an individual's unique gut environment.

For women, this could mean tailored approaches that look at hormones, stress, and gut microbe levels. Such methods might help with problems like stubborn weight gain, skin issues, or recurring urinary tract infections (UTIs). Until then, following basic guidelines on diet, rest, and stress management is the simplest way to keep gut microbes healthy.

2.11 Balancing Act

Keeping the gut in a balanced state is not about being perfect. It is about making choices that allow good microbes to grow and limiting things that feed harmful microbes. By doing this, women can help protect their bodies from a number of health problems.

If you often feel bloated, moody, or tired, it might be related to an imbalance in your gut. Paying attention to what you eat, how you manage stress, and how you care for yourself can make a difference. In the next chapters, we will talk more about hormones, stress, and other factors that shape the gut environment. Understanding these pieces can guide you toward practical steps for a healthier gut.

2.12 Closing Thoughts for Chapter 2

Microbes play a big part in our overall health, and this is especially true for women. While many of these organisms help keep us healthy, shifts in our bodies—like hormone changes or stress—can cause an imbalance. By learning how to support helpful microbes, we give our bodies the best chance to stay strong.

The next chapter will focus on hormones and their effect on digestion. This is a key area for women, as hormones can act like messengers that set off a chain of events in the gut. Knowing how this process works can help women fine-tune their eating habits, daily routines, and other parts of life to keep both gut and mind in good shape.

Chapter 3

Hormones and Digestion

Hormones are chemical messengers in the body. They move through the bloodstream and pass signals from one organ to another. Women have a unique hormone cycle that can affect energy levels, mood, and digestion. While some people may link hormones only to reproductive matters, they actually have a major impact on how the gut works. This chapter takes a detailed look at the different hormones in a woman's body and how they can change the way the digestive system behaves.

3.1 Main Hormones that Affect Digestion

1. **Estrogen**:
   Estrogen is often thought of in relation to the reproductive cycle. However, it also plays a part in gut function. When estrogen levels change, the muscles in the intestines can move more quickly or more slowly. If they move too fast, there can be diarrhea. If they move too slow, there can be constipation. Also, estrogen can affect how the gut lining repairs itself. If the lining does not repair correctly, a person might face bloating or other forms of discomfort.
2. **Progesterone**:
   Progesterone tends to rise in the second half of the menstrual cycle. High levels of progesterone can slow down the movement of the digestive tract. This is why some women experience constipation or bloating during certain times of the month. Progesterone also affects how the body stores and uses fat, which may change the type of bacteria that grows in the intestines.
3. **Cortisol**:
   Cortisol is known as a stress hormone. It is released when we feel worried or when the body senses danger. Although both men and women have cortisol, women can be more affected by stress because of monthly hormone fluctuations. High cortisol over a long time can damage the balance of gut bacteria, causing issues such as

upset stomach, frequent bowel movements, or even ulcers in severe cases.
4. **Insulin**:
Insulin helps control blood sugar levels. When insulin levels are too high or too low, blood sugar can swing up and down. This can cause energy changes that may affect what types of foods a person craves. Over time, imbalances in insulin can change the gut environment by promoting the growth of certain microbes that feed on sugar. In turn, this can affect how the body digests carbs or handles weight changes.
5. **Thyroid Hormones**:
The thyroid gland releases hormones that control how quickly the body uses energy. If the thyroid is overactive, a person may have more frequent bowel movements. If it is underactive, they might become constipated. Women are more likely to have thyroid issues than men, so it is important to be aware of this link if you notice big shifts in digestion alongside fatigue, changes in hair quality, or unexpected weight gain or loss.

3.2 The Menstrual Cycle and Gut Changes

During a typical 28-day cycle (though it can be longer or shorter for some women), the body experiences rising and falling levels of estrogen and progesterone. These changes can lead to:

- **Bloating**: Often happens before a period when hormone levels are shifting.
- **Constipation**: May occur in the second half of the cycle when progesterone is higher.
- **Loose Stools**: Some women find that when estrogen drops right before a period, they experience looser bowel movements.

For some individuals, these changes can be mild. For others, they can be quite troubling. Paying attention to digestive changes at different points in the cycle may help identify patterns. For instance, if you notice that a certain week is always linked with bloating, you can adjust your diet to help reduce that discomfort by adding more foods that support regular bowel function or by drinking more water.

3.3 Hormone Shifts Over a Lifetime

1. **Puberty**:
   Hormone levels change a lot during the teen years. Puberty can bring mood changes, skin issues, and changes in appetite. A teenager's gut may show signs of gas or bloating if diet, stress, and hormones are all shifting at once. Getting enough healthy fats, proteins, and fiber can support good gut function.
2. **Pregnancy and Postpartum**:
   During pregnancy, progesterone and estrogen rise to support the growing baby. This can slow digestion and lead to constipation or heartburn. Many women also develop new food habits, either because of cravings or a dislike of certain smells. After childbirth, hormone levels shift again, which can lead to unpredictable bowel movements. Some women find their digestion changes even more if they breastfeed. Balancing diet and staying hydrated can help during this time.
3. **Perimenopause and Menopause**:
   As a woman approaches menopause, estrogen and progesterone levels can change in erratic ways. This can alter the gut environment, sometimes leading to more frequent trips to the bathroom or a tendency toward constipation. Some women also notice changes in weight. Being mindful of diet, stress, and exercise can help manage digestive upsets. There can be a decline in muscle tone with age, which includes the muscles in the gut. Keeping physically active may support regular bowel movements.

3.4 How Hormones Affect Gut Bacteria

Gut bacteria can grow or shrink in response to hormones. For example, certain bacteria might multiply more when estrogen levels are high, while others might not. If one group takes over, it could lead to less variety in the gut. Having many types of bacteria is important for strong digestion and immunity. A less diverse set of gut bacteria can show up in signs like skin issues, frequent infections, or weight changes.

In some cases, an overgrowth of bacteria in the small intestine (SIBO) can happen. Although both men and women can get SIBO, hormone changes can raise the risk for women, especially if the normal movement of the intestines slows down. SIBO often leads to bloating, pain, and problems with absorbing nutrients. Checking with a medical professional and making changes to diet can help correct this issue.

3.5 The Role of Birth Control

Birth control pills and other hormone-based methods (patch, ring, or shot) can influence digestion. These methods often raise levels of synthetic estrogen and/or progesterone in the body to prevent pregnancy. Some women report changes in bowel habits, including more frequent constipation. Others may notice mild stomach upset or a shift in appetite.

Not everyone will experience gut changes on birth control, but if you do, it could be related to how the added hormones are affecting your body's normal balance. Some women also develop more yeast infections or urinary tract infections when on hormonal birth control, which can be tied to changes in the vaginal microbiome. If this happens, it might be helpful to discuss alternative methods or additional supplements with a healthcare professional.

3.6 Hormones and Mood in Relation to Digestion

Hormones can strongly affect mood, and mood is linked to gut function. For instance, when a woman has a sudden drop in estrogen, she might feel sad or short-tempered. This emotional strain can trigger bowel movements if the muscles in the gut tense up, or it could lead to constipation if stress slows them down. Over time, these mood and hormone changes can disrupt the balance of bacteria in the gut, creating a feedback loop that can be hard to break.

Some women find that adding foods rich in magnesium or vitamin B6 helps with mood problems around their monthly cycle. These nutrients may support hormone balance and calm the nervous system. Good sources of magnesium include nuts, seeds, dark leafy greens, and beans. Vitamin B6 can be found in foods like chickpeas, salmon, and fortified cereals.

3.7 Supporting Hormone Balance Through Food

1. **Phytochemicals**:
   Foods like soy, flaxseeds, and certain berries have plant chemicals that can mimic some aspects of estrogen. For certain women, these can be helpful if they are low in estrogen. However, for women with high estrogen, too many of these foods might not be ideal. It often helps to speak with a dietitian if you are unsure how much of these foods to include in your diet.
2. **Protein**:
   Getting enough protein is crucial, since hormones are often built from amino acids (the building blocks of protein). Good protein sources include beans, lentils, eggs, fish, and lean meats. Having a balanced intake of protein throughout the day can stabilize blood sugar, which in turn can support balanced hormone levels.
3. **Healthy Fats**:
   Hormones like estrogen and progesterone are made partly from cholesterol and other fats. Foods like avocados, nuts, and olive oil can provide healthy fats without causing major ups and downs in blood sugar. Omega-3 fatty acids, found in fish like salmon and sardines, may also support lower inflammation in the gut.
4. **Cruciferous Vegetables**:
   Vegetables such as broccoli, cauliflower, and Brussels sprouts contain substances that help the body process estrogen in a balanced way. These vegetables can promote the breakdown of excess estrogen, which might help with issues like bloating or fluid retention linked to hormone swings. However, if you have certain

thyroid conditions, too many cruciferous vegetables might not be ideal unless they are well-cooked and eaten in moderate amounts.

3.8 Lifestyle Habits that Affect Hormone Levels

1. **Sleep**:
   Sleep helps the body repair cells, regulate hormones, and clear out waste products from the brain. Women who do not get enough sleep may see imbalances in cortisol, which can interfere with estrogen and progesterone. Aim for about 7-9 hours of sleep each night. Keeping a regular bedtime can help your body maintain a stable hormone rhythm.
2. **Physical Activity**:
   Exercise can help the body use up stress hormones and keep insulin stable. Moderate activities like walking, gentle yoga (without advanced poses), or swimming can support hormone balance. Strenuous workouts might lead to short-term increases in cortisol, but in most cases, regular exercise helps the body manage stress better.
3. **Stress Management**:
   Chronic stress can cause the body to produce more cortisol, which can disrupt other hormones. This can lead to sugar cravings and poor eating habits. Finding healthy ways to lower stress can help keep hormone levels within a better range, leading to a more stable gut environment.
4. **Limiting Toxins**:
   Certain chemicals in everyday items (like plastics, cosmetics, or cleaning products) can mimic or block hormones. These substances are sometimes called "endocrine disruptors." Checking labels on products and choosing more natural options may help reduce this effect. Avoiding BPA in plastic bottles is one example of a simple change that could support better hormone health.

3.9 Checking Your Hormone Levels

If you notice ongoing digestive troubles along with problems like irregular periods, extreme mood changes, or unexplained weight gain, it might be wise to check hormone levels. A medical professional can order blood, saliva, or urine tests. These tests can show whether certain hormones are too high or too low. Knowing where you stand can help guide changes in diet or lead to further testing if needed.

Examples of hormones that might be tested include:

- Estrogen
- Progesterone
- FSH (follicle-stimulating hormone) and LH (luteinizing hormone)
- Thyroid hormones (TSH, T3, T4)
- Cortisol
- Insulin

3.10 Helpful Tips for Different Hormone-Related Situations

1. **Premenstrual Syndrome (PMS)**:
    - Increase magnesium-rich foods, like nuts and seeds.
    - Try to limit sugary snacks, as sugar spikes can worsen mood swings.
    - Stay well hydrated to reduce bloating.
2. **Menopause**:
    - Consider talking to a professional about hormone therapy if symptoms become severe.
    - Focus on protein, healthy fats, and fiber to maintain gut health and stable weight.
    - Check your calcium and vitamin D levels for bone health, which can also support muscle function in the gut.
3. **Polycystic Ovary Syndrome (PCOS)**:
    - This condition often involves insulin resistance, which can change appetite and gut function.

- A balanced diet with whole grains, fruits, vegetables, and lean protein can help keep insulin levels stable.
- Some women find that moderate exercise improves how their bodies respond to insulin.
4. **Thyroid Disorders:**
    - If you have hypothyroidism (underactive thyroid), you may experience constipation. A diet with enough fiber and water can help.
    - If you have hyperthyroidism (overactive thyroid), you may deal with frequent bathroom trips. Adjusting your diet to include enough nutrients can be important.

3.11 Avoiding Common Pitfalls

1. **Skipping Meals:**
   Skipping meals can cause blood sugar to drop, leading to mood swings and extra stress on the body's hormones. Over time, this can shift the gut environment in a negative way.
2. **Relying Too Much on Supplements:**
   While some supplements can help, they should not replace a good diet. Too many supplements can lead to imbalances, especially if you are already dealing with hormone shifts.
3. **Ignoring Persistent Symptoms:**
   Occasional bloating or cramps might be normal, but if they become constant, it is important to seek help. Hormone-related issues can sometimes be solved with small changes, but in other cases, a professional may need to get involved.

3.12 Putting It All Together

Hormones have a big impact on women's digestion. By understanding how estrogen, progesterone, cortisol, insulin, and other hormones act, you can better manage gut-related problems. Different stages of life bring distinct hormone challenges, which can influence gut bacteria and the way the stomach and intestines work. Adjusting your diet, sleep habits, and stress levels can make a big difference.

Listening to your body is key. If you track your monthly cycle and notice patterns in digestion or mood, you can plan for those times. For example, if you know you get constipated right before your period, you might add extra fiber or water a few days early. Paying attention to details can help you figure out what works and what does not.

In the next chapter, we will look deeper at stress and the digestive system. While we touched on cortisol here, we will explore in more detail how stress can change gut movement, bacteria balance, and even the brain's relationship with digestion.

Chapter 4

Stress and the Digestive System

Stress is a normal part of life. We all experience it, whether from deadlines, relationships, or unexpected problems. However, when stress becomes a constant factor, it can harm the body in many ways. One area that often takes a hit is the gut. This chapter will break down how stress and digestion are connected, why women might be more prone to stress-related gut issues, and what steps can be taken to reduce the impact of stress on the stomach and intestines.

4.1 What is Stress?

Stress happens when the body reacts to a challenge or a threat. This reaction can be helpful in small doses, motivating us to meet a deadline or avoid danger. But when stress continues for a long time, the body's stress response can stay switched on. This leads to higher levels of cortisol and other stress hormones.

Physical signs of stress might include tense muscles, rapid heartbeat, and sweaty palms. Emotional signs can be worry, sadness, anger, or feeling out of control. Over time, stress can harm the immune system, make sleep harder, and worsen gut problems like irritable bowel syndrome (IBS), ulcers, or acid reflux.

4.2 The Stress-Gut Link

1. **Blood Flow**:
   When you are stressed, the body directs blood flow away from the digestive organs. It goes instead to the muscles and brain to help you "handle" the threat. If this state lasts too long, the stomach and intestines do not get enough blood flow to do their job well. This might lead to cramps, indigestion, or slow transit times.

2. **Muscle Tension**:
   Stress can make the muscles in the gut tighter. Tense muscles might move waste through the intestines too quickly or not quickly enough, leading to diarrhea or constipation.
3. **Gut-Brain Communication**:
   The brain and gut share signals through the vagus nerve. When the brain is stressed, it sends signals that can change gut movements and the release of digestive juices. This can cause discomfort, increased acid, or changes in bowel patterns.
4. **Gut Bacteria**:
   Stress hormones can change the gut's pH levels and reduce the diversity of gut microbes. Some studies show that chronic stress can allow certain harmful bacteria to multiply. This can lead to stomach pain, bloating, or even infections.

4.3 Why Women Can Feel More Stress in the Gut

Women often handle many roles, such as work, caregiving, and household tasks. This can lead to ongoing stress. Hormone shifts can also heighten the body's response to stressful events. For example, around the time of a monthly cycle or during perimenopause, women might feel more emotional highs and lows. This can make stress feel stronger, which in turn can upset the gut.

Another factor is social expectation. Some women might feel pressured to maintain a certain appearance, juggle family duties, and succeed at work. This pressure can lead to chronic stress, which, over time, might harm the gut's natural balance. Not everyone has the same reaction to stress, but it is important to be aware of these influences.

4.4 Common Stress-Related Gut Problems

1. **Irritable Bowel Syndrome (IBS)**:
   IBS is a condition marked by cramping, bloating, gas, and irregular bowel movements (diarrhea, constipation, or both). Stress is not the

only cause, but it often makes IBS worse. Women tend to have IBS more often than men, possibly because of hormone changes and different stress responses.

2. **Acid Reflux:**
Stress can increase stomach acid or reduce the function of the muscles that keep acid out of the esophagus. The result might be heartburn or a burning sensation in the chest. If this continues, it could develop into gastroesophageal reflux disease (GERD).

3. **Ulcers:**
In some cases, chronic stress can lead to an increased risk of ulcers. While bacteria called H. pylori are often the main cause, stress might worsen an existing ulcer or slow its healing. Ulcers can cause sharp pain in the stomach, nausea, and loss of appetite.

4. **Inflammatory Bowel Disease (IBD):**
Conditions like Crohn's disease and ulcerative colitis are linked to an overactive immune response in the gut. Stress does not cause these conditions, but it can flare them up. Women with IBD might see an increase in symptoms during times of high stress.

4.5 Stress Hormones in Detail

1. **Cortisol:**
As mentioned, cortisol is released by the adrenal glands. It prepares the body to handle a challenge by raising blood sugar and limiting some processes that are not needed for immediate survival (such as digestion). Over time, too much cortisol can damage the lining of the gut, encourage harmful bacteria growth, and even weaken the immune system.

2. **Adrenaline (Epinephrine):**
This hormone boosts heart rate and directs blood flow to vital organs and muscles. While helpful in short bursts, constant adrenaline release can reduce blood flow to the gut. Some people notice they must rush to the bathroom when anxious or excited because their gut muscles contract more quickly.

3. **Norepinephrine:**
Similar to adrenaline, norepinephrine prepares the body for action. This hormone can also affect gut movement. Chronic release might

lead to irritation of the gut lining, making it more sensitive to pain or bloating.

4.6 Techniques to Lower Stress for Better Digestion

1. **Breathing Exercises**:
   Taking slow, deep breaths can help calm the nervous system. When you notice stress building, pause and take a few steady breaths in through the nose, then out through the mouth. This sends a signal to the body that it is safe, letting the parasympathetic system (the "rest and digest" system) take over.
2. **Progressive Muscle Relaxation**:
   This involves tensing and then relaxing different muscle groups. It can lower overall tension in the body, which may help the gut function better. Many people find that doing this before bedtime helps them sleep more soundly.
3. **Gentle Movement**:
   Activities like walking, stretching, or low-impact workouts can help reduce stress hormones. Movement can also support normal digestion by keeping blood flow healthy and muscles active. For women who are extra busy, even a ten-minute walk around the block can help lower stress in the gut.
4. **Guided Imagery**:
   This method uses calming images or thoughts to shift the mind away from worry. People often listen to a recording or use a script that guides them through a relaxing mental scene. This can reduce gut muscle tension and lower stress hormones.
5. **Talking to Someone**:
   Sharing worries with a friend, counselor, or support group can help process stress. Bottling up anxiety can worsen physical symptoms. Emotional support can reduce the feelings of isolation that sometimes come with ongoing stress or gut issues.

4.7 Food and Supplements for Stress Management

1. **Herbal Teas**:
   Chamomile, peppermint, and lavender teas can have a calming effect. Peppermint especially can soothe the gut muscles, which might help with mild cramps or discomfort. However, if you have acid reflux, peppermint could worsen symptoms by relaxing the valve that keeps stomach acid down, so be mindful of that.
2. **Omega-3 Fats**:
   Foods rich in omega-3 fats (like salmon, sardines, chia seeds, and walnuts) may help the body handle stress better by supporting the brain and reducing inflammation. These fats can also help the gut lining stay strong.
3. **Magnesium**:
   Known as the "relaxation mineral," magnesium supports muscle relaxation and nerve function. Good sources include leafy greens, nuts, seeds, and whole grains. Some people take a magnesium supplement before bed to help with sleep. However, taking too much can cause diarrhea, so it is wise to start small.
4. **Adaptogens**:
   Some herbs, such as ashwagandha or rhodiola, are said to help the body cope with stress. Women should check with a medical professional before using these, especially if they are pregnant, breastfeeding, or on birth control, because adaptogens can sometimes interact with hormone levels.
5. **Probiotics**:
   Since stress can alter gut bacteria, probiotics might be helpful in restoring balance. These can be found in foods like yogurt, kefir, and fermented vegetables. A high-quality probiotic supplement might also be considered. Look for one with strains that have been studied for stress or mood support, such as certain Bifidobacterium or Lactobacillus strains.

4.8 Setting Boundaries

Sometimes, stress comes from having too much on your plate. Learning to set boundaries with work, family, or friends can be a major step toward better mental health. If you often agree to extra tasks when you are already overwhelmed, you may build up stress without noticing. Over time, that stress can harm your gut. Setting boundaries might mean saying "no" to certain events or tasks, or asking for help when you need it.

4.9 Tracking Stress-Related Digestive Symptoms

If you suspect that stress is messing with your gut, keeping a simple log can help. You can note:

- The time of day and what you were doing
- Stress level (maybe on a scale of 1 to 10)
- Any stomach issues (cramps, bloating, diarrhea, constipation)
- Foods eaten around that time

After a few weeks, patterns might emerge. For example, you may notice you get heartburn after a tough meeting at work. Or you might see you wake up with a stomachache on days when you have a big exam or presentation. Knowing these patterns can help you take steps to lower stress or adjust your schedule to avoid triggers.

4.10 Breathing for the Vagus Nerve

The vagus nerve is a key player in the gut-brain connection. It helps regulate heart rate, digestion, and certain reflexes like gagging. Stress can cause the vagus nerve to become less active, leading to slower gut function or more discomfort. Deep breathing is a simple way to increase vagus nerve activity. Some people also try humming or gargling with water for a few seconds, which can stimulate the back of the throat and help the vagus nerve.

4.11 When to Seek Professional Help

If you are experiencing persistent stress that leads to severe digestive issues, it might be time to talk to a healthcare provider. They might suggest therapy for stress management, medication to reduce anxiety, or further tests to rule out ulcers or other gut problems. There is no need to face chronic stress alone. Often, professional help can bring improvements in digestion and mental wellbeing.

You may also want to see a gut specialist (like a gastroenterologist) if you have:

- Unexplained weight loss
- Rectal bleeding
- Severe or constant pain
- A family history of serious digestive diseases

In these cases, stress might be part of the picture, but there could be other medical factors that need attention.

4.12 Building a Personalized Stress-Reduction Plan

1. **Identify Stress Triggers**:
   Make a list of things that regularly cause stress. This might include work deadlines, relationship problems, or health worries.
2. **Choose Coping Methods**:
   Pick from the techniques mentioned earlier—breathing exercises, gentle movement, therapy, or dietary changes—to see which ones fit into your life.
3. **Set Small Goals**:
   Rather than trying to fix all stress at once, focus on one area at a time. For example, start by adding a five-minute morning relaxation routine.
4. **Evaluate Progress**:
   After a week or two, check if your gut feels better. Are you having fewer stomach problems? Are you more relaxed? If something is not helping, try a different approach.

This process can help you find what works best for your body. Everyone's stress triggers and lifestyles are different, so a plan that helps one person might not help another.

4.13 Workplace Stress and Gut Health

Many women spend a large part of their day at work. Tight deadlines, long hours, or conflicts with coworkers can increase stress. Here are a few ideas to reduce workplace stress:

- **Take Short Breaks**: Every hour or so, stand up, stretch, or walk around. Moving your body can reset the mind and help the gut stay active.
- **Hydration**: Keep a water bottle at your desk. Dehydration can worsen stress and lead to constipation.
- **Healthy Snacks**: Try to have balanced snacks on hand, such as fruit, nuts, or yogurt. Avoid too many sugary treats or caffeine, which can spike stress hormones.
- **Talk to Management**: If your workload is too heavy, consider speaking with a supervisor about ways to redistribute tasks.

4.14 Family and Emotional Stress

Family life can sometimes be demanding, especially for women who juggle responsibilities for children, elderly parents, or partners. The emotional strain can lead to stress-related gut issues. Setting routines for meals, bedtimes, and chores can bring order to a busy household. Clear communication with family members about your needs can also reduce tension. If conflict arises often, family counseling might be an option.

4.15 Stress, Sleep, and Digestion

When stress is high, sleep can suffer. Lack of rest can harm the gut by throwing off the body's internal clock. The digestive system relies on daily rhythms to release enzymes and move food along. A healthy sleep schedule supports better bowel movements and more balanced gut bacteria.

- **Create a Bedtime Routine**: This might include reading, listening to soft music, or having a warm bath. Avoid bright screens or heavy meals close to bedtime.
- **Room Environment**: Keep the room quiet, dark, and at a comfortable temperature. Earplugs or a sleep mask can be helpful if your environment is not ideal.
- **Limit Stimulants**: Avoid caffeinated drinks in the late afternoon or evening.

4.16 Stress and Body Weight Changes

Stress can cause some people to gain weight and others to lose it. When stressed, some may crave sugary or fatty foods for comfort, which can harm gut bacteria over time. Others might lose their appetite. Sudden weight changes can upset the balance in the gut, leading to problems like bloating, diarrhea, or constipation.

Keeping a balanced diet and trying to maintain stable eating habits can help. Planning meals ahead of time and prepping healthy snacks can limit last-minute fast food decisions that could worsen gut health.

4.17 Myths About Stress and the Gut

- **Myth: Stress is the only cause of ulcers.**
  While stress can worsen ulcers, a bacteria called H. pylori or certain medicines (like NSAIDs) often cause them.

- **Myth: Only high-stress jobs affect digestion.**
  Stress can come from many sources, such as home life or personal issues. Any type of ongoing stress can affect the gut.
- **Myth: Having no stress is the goal.**
  It is nearly impossible to have zero stress. The aim is to manage stress so it does not become overwhelming.

4.18 Supporting Yourself Through Changes

Making changes to how you handle stress is not always easy. It can take time to notice improvements in your gut. However, even small steps can help, such as practicing gentle breathing each morning or cutting back on tasks that are not essential. Rewarding yourself with something simple (like a quiet moment with a cup of tea or a short walk in nature) can make the process more pleasant. This does not mean "celebrating" in a grand sense—just creating small pleasant moments.

4.19 Balancing Stress for Better Long-Term Health

Managing stress is an ongoing process. As life changes—through marriage, children, career shifts, or health issues—your stress plan may need to adjust. By staying aware of how stress affects your digestion, you can respond more quickly to problems. This might include ramping up your relaxation methods during tough times or seeking professional help if problems become too large to handle alone.

Over time, better stress management can also support a stronger immune system, stable mood, and improved overall wellbeing. When the mind is calm, the gut has a better chance to carry out its tasks in a smooth way.

4.20 Conclusion to Chapter 4

Stress can have a powerful effect on the digestive system. From changing gut movements to shifting the balance of bacteria, ongoing stress can make daily life uncomfortable. Women, who often face multiple roles and hormone changes, might experience these effects more strongly. However, there are ways to tackle this issue, such as breathing techniques, boundary-setting, better sleep habits, and targeted food choices.

By lowering stress in daily life and supporting the body with healthy routines, you may see improvements in symptoms like bloating, cramps, or irregular bowel movements. In the next chapters, we will explore more about common digestive concerns, the brain-gut connection, and how certain foods and habits can help keep your gut in good shape for the long term.

Chapter 5

Common Digestive Concerns in Women

Women can experience various digestive troubles that cause daily discomfort, changes in eating habits, and challenges in maintaining a healthy routine. Some of these concerns happen more often in women than in men. Each person's body is unique, so the same condition may show up differently from one woman to another. This chapter looks at common problems like irritable bowel syndrome, constipation, bloating, diarrhea, acid reflux, and more. It also offers ideas on how to handle these concerns without repeating the same basic steps found elsewhere.

5.1 Irritable Bowel Syndrome (IBS)

What It Is
Irritable bowel syndrome is a condition marked by ongoing belly pain or discomfort, along with changes in bowel habits. A person with IBS may have diarrhea, constipation, or both. IBS does not lead to permanent damage in the intestines, but it can lower a person's quality of life if not managed well.

Why It's Common in Women
Women are more likely than men to be diagnosed with IBS. Reasons include hormonal changes that affect the speed of gut movements. Stress levels may also play a role, as discussed in previous chapters. For some women, IBS symptoms might be more noticeable around the time of their menstrual cycle.

Signs and Clues

- Pain or cramps in the lower stomach area
- Sudden urges to use the bathroom
- Bloating and gas
- Changes in stool consistency (hard, watery, or both)
- Feeling like you have not fully emptied your bowels

Ways to Manage IBS

- **Identify Trigger Foods**: Common triggers include fatty foods, caffeine, alcohol, onions, garlic, and high-fructose fruits. Keeping a log of what you eat and how you feel afterward can uncover patterns.
- **Fiber Balance**: Some forms of IBS benefit from more fiber, while others do not. Soluble fiber (like oats, apples, and chia seeds) is often gentler on the gut than insoluble fiber (like wheat bran).
- **Hydration**: Drinking enough water can help with both constipation and diarrhea.
- **Mindful Eating**: Eating slowly and chewing well can reduce the stress on your gut. Rushed meals often lead to more gas and bloating.
- **Stress Relief**: Techniques like slow breathing or light stretching can help, since stress can set off IBS flare-ups.

5.2 Constipation

Definition
Constipation happens when bowel movements become less frequent or difficult to pass. A person might go days without a normal bowel movement. Stools can become hard or dry, making them painful to pass.

Why It Happens More Often in Women
Hormonal swings, especially higher levels of progesterone, can slow down gut movement. This is common during the second half of the menstrual cycle or early in pregnancy. Additionally, some women may not drink enough fluids or eat enough fiber each day, which can worsen constipation.

Key Causes

- Low fiber intake
- Not drinking enough water
- Inactive lifestyle
- Ignoring the urge to go
- Certain medications (like certain painkillers or iron supplements)

- Thyroid issues (an underactive thyroid can lead to slower movements)

Practical Tips

- **Fiber-Rich Foods**: Beans, lentils, berries, pears, oats, and whole-grain products can help. Gradually increase fiber to avoid gas.
- **Hydration**: Aim for water or herbal teas throughout the day.
- **Regular Movement**: A daily walk or light exercise can stimulate bowel activity.
- **Scheduled Bathroom Time**: Some women find that setting aside a consistent time each day helps train the body to go more regularly.
- **Stool Softeners or Mild Laxatives**: These can be used occasionally, but it is best to speak with a healthcare professional if constipation is ongoing.

5.3 Bloating and Gas

Causes of Bloating
Bloating can happen for many reasons, from eating certain foods to swallowing air. Hormonal changes during a menstrual cycle can also make a woman feel more swollen or puffy in the belly region.

Foods That May Lead to Gas

- Beans and lentils
- Cruciferous vegetables (like broccoli, cabbage, and Brussels sprouts)
- Carbonated drinks
- Chewing gum (due to swallowing air)

Tips to Reduce Bloating

- **Slow Down**: Eating too fast can increase the amount of air you swallow. This can lead to bloating.
- **Cook Vegetables Well**: Cooking can make high-fiber vegetables easier to handle.

- **Try Herbal Teas**: Some women find that peppermint or fennel tea (unless reflux is an issue) eases gas.
- **Be Aware of Sugar Substitutes**: Products containing sorbitol, mannitol, or xylitol can lead to gas for some individuals.

5.4 Diarrhea

Overview
Diarrhea involves loose, watery stools that might occur often throughout the day. It can be acute (short-lived) or chronic (lasting more than four weeks). Women might face diarrhea around certain times in their menstrual cycle or when under high stress.

Common Causes

- Viral or bacterial infections
- Food intolerances (e.g., lactose intolerance)
- Stress or anxiety
- Side effects of medication
- Certain supplements (like high doses of magnesium)

Helpful Measures

- **Stay Hydrated**: Diarrhea causes a loss of fluids and electrolytes. Sipping water or oral rehydration solutions can prevent dehydration.
- **Gentle Foods**: Plain rice, bananas, applesauce, and toast are often recommended. They are easy on the stomach.
- **Limit Spicy or Fatty Foods**: These can worsen diarrhea.
- **Consider Probiotics**: Some strains of beneficial bacteria may help restore balance in the gut faster.

5.5 Acid Reflux and GERD

What It Is
Acid reflux is when stomach acid goes back up into the esophagus, causing a burning feeling in the chest (known as heartburn). Gastroesophageal reflux disease (GERD) is a more long-lasting form of this issue. It can harm the lining of the esophagus over time.

Women's Risk Factors
Pregnancy can raise the chance of acid reflux because the growing uterus can push the stomach upward. Hormones may also relax the valve between the stomach and esophagus, making reflux more likely. Stress can add to this condition by increasing stomach acid or tightening certain muscles.

Signs

- Burning feeling in the chest, especially after eating or lying down
- A sour or bitter taste in the mouth
- Trouble swallowing
- Feeling like there is a lump in the throat

Prevention and Relief

- **Smaller Meals**: Eating large meals can lead to too much pressure on the valve, causing acid to rise.
- **Avoid Lying Down Right After Eating**: Wait at least two to three hours before going to bed.
- **Limit Certain Triggers**: Common triggers include caffeine, alcohol, tomato-based foods, chocolate, and spicy dishes.
- **Raise the Head of the Bed**: Sleeping with the head slightly elevated can help keep acid in the stomach.

5.6 Small Intestinal Bacterial Overgrowth (SIBO)

Definition
SIBO happens when too many bacteria grow in the small intestine. Normally, most bacteria live in the large intestine. When they grow in the

small intestine, they can cause bloating, diarrhea, or nutrient absorption issues.

Why Women May Be More Susceptible
Hormonal shifts, certain types of birth control, or slower gut movements can create conditions that allow bacteria to grow in the wrong place. Stress and certain medicines may also set the stage for SIBO.

Possible Signs

- Excessive bloating soon after eating
- Pain in the upper abdomen
- A feeling of fullness quickly when eating
- Changes in bowel movements (either diarrhea or constipation)

Approach

- **Testing**: A doctor might suggest a breath test to confirm SIBO.
- **Diet**: Some individuals follow a specific eating plan (often low in fermentable carbs) to lower bacteria growth.
- **Antibiotics**: Certain antibiotics or antimicrobials may help reduce bacterial overgrowth.
- **Prokinetics**: These medicines help move food through the gut at a normal pace, preventing bacteria from lingering.

5.7 Pelvic Floor Dysfunction

Link to Digestion
The pelvic floor is a group of muscles that support organs in the lower abdomen. Problems with these muscles can show up as urinary incontinence or pain. But they can also affect how stool passes. If the muscles cannot relax properly, a woman might feel constipated or strain a lot during bowel movements.

Causes

- Childbirth can weaken or injure pelvic floor muscles.

- Frequent straining due to constipation can put pressure on these muscles over time.
- Certain surgeries or injuries may play a role as well.

Possible Solutions

- **Physical Therapy**: Working with a trained therapist can help strengthen or retrain the pelvic floor muscles.
- **Biofeedback**: Sensors can show how well a person is contracting or relaxing these muscles, helping them learn better control.
- **Diet Changes**: Solving chronic constipation can reduce strain on the pelvic floor.

5.8 Gallbladder and Liver-Related Digestive Issues

Gallbladder Problems

Gallstones can cause sudden pain in the upper-right side of the abdomen, especially after eating a fatty meal. Women are more likely to get gallstones due to factors like hormone changes, pregnancy, or certain diets.

Liver Stress

While the liver is involved in many processes, chronic stress, poor diets, or alcohol use can lead to issues that affect digestion. The liver produces bile that helps break down fats. If there is a disruption, you might see changes in stool color or texture.

Possible Steps

- **Balance Fat Intake**: Extreme high-fat or low-fat diets can cause issues in how bile is released.
- **Stay Hydrated**: This helps all organs function better, including the gallbladder.
- **Consider Medical Tests**: If you have sudden or severe pain, an ultrasound may identify gallstones or other problems.

5.9 Food Intolerances and Sensitivities

What They Are
An intolerance means the body lacks certain enzymes to break down a specific component of food. For example, lactose intolerance is when the body does not produce enough lactase to digest dairy. A sensitivity involves a negative reaction that is not always well-understood by standard tests.

Common Types

- Lactose (milk sugar)
- Gluten (protein in wheat, barley, and rye)
- Fructose (fruit sugar)
- Histamines (found in aged or fermented foods)

Managing Them

- **Keep a Food Diary**: Track meals and symptoms to see if a pattern emerges.
- **Testing**: A hydrogen breath test might show if you have lactose or fructose intolerance. Blood tests can check for celiac disease.
- **Gradual Elimination**: Removing a suspect food for a short time and then trying it again can help you see if it causes problems.

5.10 The Impact of Medications

Overview
Some medicines can irritate the lining of the stomach or slow gut movement. Others might speed up movements. Women, who might take birth control, hormone replacement therapy, or certain painkillers, could face extra challenges.

Examples

- **Nonsteroidal Anti-Inflammatory Drugs (NSAIDs)**: Long-term use can damage the stomach lining.
- **Opioid Painkillers**: Commonly cause constipation.
- **Iron Supplements**: Known for causing constipation and dark stools.

- **Antibiotics**: Can kill healthy gut bacteria, leading to diarrhea or yeast overgrowth.

What to Do

- **Speak with Your Healthcare Provider**: They might adjust the dose or suggest ways to reduce side effects.
- **Take Probiotics**: Particularly after a course of antibiotics to help restore gut balance.
- **Stay Attentive**: If a medication is causing severe discomfort, do not ignore it.

5.11 Stress and Anxiety in Digestive Disorders

Although we covered stress in detail in the previous chapter, it is worth noting again that conditions like IBS, reflux, and even constipation can get worse with anxiety. When the body is tense, the muscles in the digestive tract can overreact or underreact. If you notice your stomach feels off during stressful periods, consider a daily relaxation exercise or mild physical activity to help release tension.

5.12 Lesser-Known Digestive Issues

1. **Endometriosis-Related Gut Pain**
   Endometriosis causes tissue that resembles the uterine lining to grow outside the uterus. It can attach to parts of the digestive tract, causing pain, diarrhea, or constipation, especially during menstrual cycles. Some women mistake these symptoms for IBS. Proper diagnosis often requires special imaging or surgery to look inside.
2. **Gastroparesis**
   This is a condition where the stomach empties more slowly than normal. It can cause feelings of fullness after just a few bites, as well as bloating, nausea, and sometimes vomiting. While it is not as common, women might be at higher risk if they have certain autoimmune disorders or diabetes.

3. **Bile Acid Diarrhea**
   This happens when bile acids from the liver are not properly absorbed in the small intestine and move into the large intestine, triggering watery stools. Sometimes it is caused by issues in the gallbladder or after certain types of surgery.

5.13 When to Seek Medical Advice

Many digestive problems can be managed with small changes to diet or lifestyle. However, it is important to contact a healthcare professional if you see signs such as:

- Blood in the stool
- Ongoing and severe stomach pain
- Unplanned weight loss
- Unusual fatigue or weakness
- Frequent vomiting or nausea

It can help to keep a record of symptoms and note any patterns. This information can assist the doctor in figuring out the cause. In some cases, tests like colonoscopies, endoscopies, or imaging may be needed to take a closer look at what is happening inside the digestive tract.

5.14 How Emotions Can Hide as Digestive Problems

Some women carry tension in their bodies without realizing it. Anxiety, sadness, or anger might show up as bloating, cramps, or frequent bathroom trips. If this is the case, addressing the emotional side might help the body relax and relieve some digestive problems. Therapy, counseling, or support groups can be valuable in sorting out emotions that could be playing a hidden role in how the gut feels.

5.15 Building a Strong Foundation

Many of these common digestive concerns share similar lifestyle factors:

- **Eating Patterns**: Balanced meals with enough fiber, protein, and healthy fats can support smoother digestion.
- **Stress Management**: Chronic tension can worsen any gut problem.
- **Exercise**: Helps promote regular movements and overall health.
- **Hydration**: Supports bowel function and helps flush out waste.
- **Adequate Sleep**: The body resets overnight, which can help with hormone regulation and gut repair.

Focusing on these basic habits can prevent some concerns from showing up or at least reduce how severe they become.

5.16 Digging Deeper with Tests and Exams

If a digestive concern is not improving, certain tests might help:

- **Endoscopy**: Looks inside the upper digestive tract.
- **Colonoscopy**: Views the large intestine.
- **Stool Analysis**: Checks for hidden blood, excess fat, or microbes.
- **Breath Tests**: Used for lactose intolerance, fructose intolerance, or SIBO.
- **Food Sensitivity Panels**: Though these can be controversial, they sometimes offer clues about certain triggers.

5.17 Avoiding Repeat Mistakes

It is easy to slip back into old patterns when a gut issue starts to calm down. But if you have discovered that certain foods or habits cause problems, it is wise to keep them in check for the long term. For instance, if you know dairy triggers bloating, set clear rules about when and how much you consume. If you slip up now and then, that is normal, but a general plan will help you avoid big flare-ups.

5.18 Women's Groups and Support Networks

Sometimes, connecting with others who have similar digestive troubles can offer more than just emotional support. You can learn helpful tips or find out about specialists in your area. Online forums, local meetups, and social media groups exist for many of these conditions. While you should be careful with unverified health claims, you may find new ideas to discuss with your healthcare provider.

5.19 Considering Alternative Approaches

A few women look into acupuncture, massage therapy, or certain traditional practices for digestion support. While evidence can be mixed, some individuals do report relief. If you choose these methods, try to see a certified practitioner and keep your usual doctor informed. Integrating alternative approaches can sometimes fill in gaps not covered by standard treatments, but safety should always come first.

5.20 Conclusion to Chapter 5

Common digestive concerns in women can range from IBS and constipation to acid reflux and food sensitivities. These problems might happen more often or be more intense than in men due to hormone shifts, stress, and other lifestyle factors. Yet there are many ways to manage them, from adjusting diet and exercise to seeking specialized care when needed.

The next chapter will discuss the brain-gut connection in more depth. While it has been mentioned in previous parts of the book, it is worth taking a closer look at how the brain and gut talk to each other and how this relationship can impact everything from mood to appetite. With a clearer picture of how these signals work, women can be better equipped to handle both the mental and physical sides of digestive health.

Chapter 6

The Brain-Gut Connection

Many people have heard the phrase "gut feeling." This simple phrase hints at a deeper reality: the brain and the gut communicate constantly. Thoughts and emotions can affect digestion, while signals from the stomach and intestines can influence mood and thinking. This chapter explores how that connection works and why it matters so much for women's health.

6.1 How the Brain and Gut Talk to Each Other

1. **Nervous System Pathways**:
   The vagus nerve is a key highway that carries signals between the brain and gut. It can sense factors like how full the stomach is and send updates back to the brain. In return, the brain sends signals that affect muscle contraction in the intestines, acid release in the stomach, and other important tasks.
2. **Chemical Messengers**:
   These are substances like serotonin, dopamine, and gamma-aminobutyric acid (GABA). Though commonly linked to mood or behavior in the brain, a large portion of serotonin, for instance, is produced in the gut. Imbalances in these messengers can affect both how a person feels emotionally and how well the gut operates.
3. **Immune System**:
   The gut houses most of our immune cells. When the gut lining is irritated, immune signals can travel to the brain, influencing mood or energy levels. At the same time, stress or worry can increase inflammation in the gut, leading to a back-and-forth loop of discomfort.

6.2 Emotions and Digestion

Anxiety and Fear
When you feel anxious or scared, your body produces stress hormones (like cortisol and adrenaline). These hormones tell the digestive system to slow down or speed up, depending on the situation. Some people might need to rush to the bathroom, while others may feel their stomach is in knots.

Sadness and Low Mood
During times of sadness, the appetite might change. Some people eat more, while others eat less. The gut might also move more slowly in the case of mild depression, leading to constipation.

Excitement and Happiness
Positive emotions can help the body release chemicals that support healthy digestion. For example, feeling calm can activate the parasympathetic system (often called "rest and digest"), which allows the gut to do its job without being interrupted by stress signals.

6.3 The Second Brain Concept

Scientists sometimes call the gut the "second brain" because it has a complex network of nerves known as the enteric nervous system. This system can function on its own, without direct orders from the brain, though it still shares signals with it. The enteric nervous system helps direct muscle movement in the intestines and regulate secretions that break down food.

Why It Matters for Women
Hormone fluctuations can affect both the main brain and the enteric nervous system. This is why some women experience digestive changes tied to emotional swings or monthly cycles. If the second brain is out of sync with the main brain, it could lead to repeated bouts of stomach pain, diarrhea, or constipation.

6.4 The Role of Serotonin

Serotonin is best known as a mood stabilizer. However, almost all of it is made in the gut. It influences bowel movements and can cause the gut to contract more or less. In some conditions like IBS, serotonin might be poorly regulated, leading to cramps, changes in stool consistency, and discomfort.

When a person takes certain antidepressants known as SSRIs (selective serotonin reuptake inhibitors), they might notice changes in digestive patterns. This is because increasing serotonin in the brain also impacts serotonin in the gut. Women who are on these medications for depression or anxiety should watch for side effects such as diarrhea or altered bowel habits.

6.5 Gut Bacteria and the Brain

The trillions of bacteria in the gut are not idle passengers. They help make or process certain substances that can reach the brain. Some strains can produce chemicals that support calmness or reduce inflammation. Others may create substances that lead to anxiety-like feelings.

Impact of Diet
What a person eats can shape which bacteria grow. For instance, diets high in processed sugar can encourage certain microbes that might lead to more inflammation or changes in mood. On the other hand, a balanced diet rich in fiber and healthy fats can promote bacteria that release calming or protective chemicals. Women who notice shifts in mood after eating certain foods might be experiencing these microbe-based effects.

6.6 Why Women May Feel the Connection More Strongly

1. **Hormone Interactions**:
   Estrogen and progesterone can affect nerve signals in the gut.

When these hormones shift quickly, women may notice more intense mood changes that also show up as digestive symptoms.
2. **Social Roles and Stress**:
If a woman balances many tasks—work, home, caregiving—chronic stress can develop. Chronic stress can weaken the signals that keep the gut calm, raising the chance of problems like IBS or reflux.
3. **Life Stages**:
Stages such as pregnancy or menopause bring sudden changes in hormone levels. These can cause new or different emotional states, which may ripple into digestive patterns.

6.7 Signs of a Brain-Gut Imbalance

- **Chronic Bloating or Discomfort** that comes and goes with mood changes
- **Frequent Bathroom Trips** when anxious
- **Constipation or Diarrhea** linked to stress or strong emotions
- **Feeling Sick to the Stomach** under pressure or sadness
- **Appetite Swings** during emotional highs or lows

Recognizing these patterns can be the first step in addressing them. If a person sees that emotional stress always sets off a gut reaction, then focusing on mental health might reduce the physical symptoms too.

6.8 Ways to Support Brain-Gut Harmony

1. **Relaxation Techniques**:
    - **Breath Work**: Slow, controlled breathing can switch on the parasympathetic system.
    - **Progressive Muscle Relaxation**: Helps release tension from the entire body, including the abdominal area.
2. **Mindful Eating**:
    - **Focus on Each Bite**: This can slow the pace of a meal and help the gut prepare properly for digestion.

- **Observe Hunger and Fullness**: Listening to the body's signals can prevent overeating or skipping meals, both of which can strain the brain-gut link.
3. **Regular Movement**:
    - **Light Exercise**: Activities like walking, swimming, or gentle yoga can lower stress hormones.
    - **Stretching**: Helps relax tense muscles around the abdomen and improves overall circulation.
4. **Balanced Nutrition**:
    - **Fiber**: Feeds beneficial gut bacteria, which can help create mood-supporting chemicals.
    - **Protein and Healthy Fats**: Support hormone production and stable energy levels.
    - **Probiotics**: In foods like kefir, yogurt, or fermented vegetables may help foster a gut environment that sends more calming signals to the brain.

6.9 Gut Feelings and Decision Making

Some research suggests that gut signals can guide choices beyond basic hunger and fullness. For example, a sudden uneasy feeling might be the body's subtle warning that something is off. While not every "gut feeling" is correct, paying attention to these signals can sometimes give an extra layer of insight. However, women who have gut imbalances might find these signals misleading until the underlying issues are resolved.

6.10 Gut Inflammation and Mood

Inflammation in the gut can lead to more than physical pain or bloating. It can also affect mood by triggering the immune system to release chemicals that reach the brain. Long-term inflammation has been linked to a higher risk of mood swings and low mood. Addressing gut inflammation through an anti-inflammatory diet, stress reduction, and sometimes specific supplements can help improve both physical and emotional wellness.

Causes of Gut Inflammation

- Unbalanced diet high in refined sugar or processed foods
- Ongoing stress
- Certain infections that damage the gut lining
- Overuse of NSAIDs (nonsteroidal anti-inflammatory drugs)
- Untreated food sensitivities

6.11 How Sleep Links the Brain and Gut

A lack of sleep can disturb hormone balance, affect hunger signals, and reduce the gut's ability to repair at night. Poor sleep can also lead to higher stress hormones, which further affect digestion. Women with insomnia or frequent night wakings might see an increase in IBS symptoms or acid reflux. Working on sleep hygiene—like having a consistent bedtime, avoiding large meals before bed, and limiting screen time late at night—can support both the brain and gut.

6.12 Postpartum Changes in the Brain-Gut Connection

After giving birth, hormone levels shift dramatically. New mothers may experience mood changes (often called "the baby blues" or, in more serious cases, postpartum depression). These mood states can lead to appetite changes or irregular bowel movements. Combined with the stress of caring for a newborn, it can upset the balance of gut bacteria. Prioritizing help from family or friends, rest, and gentle forms of self-care can support better gut function during this transition.

6.13 Brain-Gut Science: Current Findings and Future Possibilities

- **Microbial Influence**: Research is exploring how certain bacteria might help with conditions like anxiety or depression.

- **Fecal Microbiota Transplant**: This is an experimental procedure where healthy bacteria from one person's stool is placed into another person's colon. It is mainly used for severe bacterial infections at this time, but future studies may expand to mood or digestive conditions.
- **Gut-Brain Therapies**: Certain forms of talk therapy (like cognitive behavioral therapy) have shown promise in helping IBS symptoms, likely by altering how stress is handled and how signals move between the brain and gut.

6.14 Real-Life Scenarios

1. **Stressful Work Deadline**
    - A woman with IBS might notice more frequent trips to the bathroom during this time. By practicing breathing exercises each morning and keeping fiber intake consistent, she might lower the chance of a flare-up.
2. **Sudden Anxiety Before Public Speaking**
    - This can set off acid reflux or nausea. Drinking water and doing a brief relaxation routine might help calm both the mind and stomach.
3. **Late-Night Snacking After a Hard Day**
    - Emotional eating can lead to bloating or discomfort, especially if high-fat or sugary items are chosen. Finding a better emotional outlet—like journaling or gentle stretching—could reduce this habit.

6.15 The Power of Self-Awareness

Self-awareness means noticing how your body feels and what triggers certain reactions. If you find your gut acts up every time you argue with a friend or partner, you can plan to manage the stress in a healthier way. Maybe that means a short walk after a tense discussion, a phone call with a supportive person, or a few minutes of mindful breathing. By connecting mental states to physical symptoms, you can take action sooner.

6.16 When Professional Support is Needed

A strong brain-gut link can sometimes become a problem if emotional stress is severe. Signs that professional support might be needed include:

- Panic attacks or extreme worry that disrupts daily life
- Ongoing sadness or hopelessness that lasts more than a couple of weeks
- Sudden weight loss or major appetite changes that do not improve
- Abdominal pain that does not go away, even with basic stress management and diet changes

Mental health professionals can offer therapy, coping strategies, or medication if needed. Gastroenterologists can run tests to see if there is an underlying physical cause, such as ulcers or IBD. Some clinics now offer integrated care, where mental health providers and gut specialists work together.

6.17 Practical Tools for Day-to-Day Life

1. **Timer Method:**
   Set aside five or ten minutes twice a day for a calm break. During this time, do some slow breathing or a simple mindfulness exercise. This can reduce stress hormones and help the gut.
2. **Boundaries Around Media:**
   Constant doomscrolling or reading distressing news can amplify stress signals. Limiting screen time, especially before bed, can calm the mind and gut.
3. **Listening to Soothing Sounds:**
   Some women find that calm music or nature sounds can relax the body. This might be beneficial after a hectic day to help the gut settle.
4. **Posture Check:**
   Sitting up straight can support better digestion and reduce pressure on the abdomen. Slouching might compress organs and slow the movement of food through the intestines.

6.18 Hormonal Birth Control and Mood-Gut Signals

Hormonal birth control can change the balance of chemicals in the body and might alter mood in some women. This shift can also affect gut movements or the types of bacteria that thrive. If a woman notices new digestive issues after starting a new birth control method, she might want to consult with her healthcare provider about whether a different approach would be better for her body and mind.

6.19 Gender Differences in Brain-Gut Research

Studies suggest that women's brains and guts respond somewhat differently to stress and emotional triggers than men's do. For instance, women may be more prone to rumination (dwelling on a problem in thought), which can keep stress levels high. This prolonged stress might have a bigger impact on the gut. Future research will hopefully uncover more detailed ways to help women manage stress-related gut issues.

6.20 Conclusion to Chapter 6

The brain-gut connection is a two-way street. Emotional states can change how the gut functions, and imbalances in the gut can affect thoughts and feelings. Understanding this relationship can help women take better care of both mental and physical health. By focusing on stress reduction, mindful eating, gut-friendly foods, and listening to body signals, it is possible to create a steadier link between the mind and the digestive system.

In the next chapters, we will look deeper at nutrients, prebiotics, probiotics, and how specific foods can either help or hurt gut health. Building on what you have learned about the brain-gut connection, you will see how the right choices can shape your inner ecosystem and, in turn, support both digestive comfort and mental wellbeing.

Chapter 7

Nutrients for a Healthy Gut

A strong digestive system depends on a variety of nutrients. Many people know that vitamins and minerals are important, but they might not realize how these substances directly affect the stomach and intestines. Different stages of a woman's life can require different amounts of these nutrients. In this chapter, we will look at proteins, carbohydrates, fats, vitamins, and minerals that support the health of the gut. We will also explore how these nutrients work together and why some are especially important for women.

7.1 Overview of Major Nutrients

1. Proteins
Proteins are made up of amino acids. Amino acids help build and repair tissues throughout the body, including the lining of the gut. They also make enzymes and hormones that guide digestion. Getting enough protein is important for maintaining muscle mass, which includes the smooth muscle in the intestines that pushes food along.

2. Carbohydrates
Carbohydrates are the body's main source of energy. They include sugars, starches, and fiber. Fiber is a special kind of carbohydrate that does not get fully digested. Instead, it passes into the colon and supports healthy bacteria. Different types of fiber can either add bulk to stools or feed beneficial microbes.

3. Fats
Fats help the body absorb certain vitamins and produce hormones. They also provide energy. Not all fats are equal, though. Some can harm the body if eaten in high amounts, while others support cell structure. Getting the right balance of fats can help reduce inflammation in the gut.

4. Vitamins
Vitamins are organic compounds that the body needs in small amounts. They help with tasks like converting food into energy, forming red blood

cells, and maintaining immune function. A lack of certain vitamins can weaken the gut lining or reduce the body's defense against harmful bacteria.

5. Minerals

Minerals like iron, calcium, magnesium, and zinc are inorganic elements that support many body processes. For example, magnesium helps with muscle relaxation, which can aid in bowel regularity. Zinc helps with tissue repair, which is important for keeping the intestinal lining healthy.

7.2 The Role of Vitamins in Gut Health

1. **Vitamin A**
   - **Uses**: Helps maintain the health of the lining of the stomach and intestines. It also supports immune cells.
   - **Sources**: Carrots, sweet potatoes, spinach, and squash. Animal products like liver and eggs are also good sources.
   - **Notes for Women**: Women who do not get enough vitamin A might see slower repair of the gut lining or be more prone to infections. However, too much vitamin A from supplements can be harmful, so it is best to aim for balanced intake through foods.
2. **Vitamin B Complex**
   - **Common Types**: B1 (thiamine), B2 (riboflavin), B3 (niacin), B6 (pyridoxine), B9 (folate), and B12 (cobalamin).
   - **Uses**: These vitamins help turn food into energy and support the nervous system. B6, in particular, is linked to hormone balance. B12 and folate support red blood cell production, which helps transport oxygen to gut cells.
   - **Sources**: Whole grains, beans, lentils, leafy greens, eggs, milk, and meat.
   - **Notes for Women**: Low B12 can lead to fatigue and poor digestion. Women who follow a plant-based diet may need to look for B12-fortified foods or a supplement.
3. **Vitamin C**
   - **Uses**: Supports the immune system and helps the body absorb iron. It also plays a part in collagen formation, which

is important for healthy tissues, including the intestinal lining.
- **Sources**: Citrus fruits, strawberries, bell peppers, and broccoli.
- **Notes for Women**: Vitamin C can help reduce inflammation. Since women may lose blood monthly, they need to ensure healthy iron levels. Vitamin C helps with iron absorption, so it can indirectly support oxygen supply to the gut.

4. **Vitamin D**
   - **Uses**: Helps the body absorb calcium and may also support gut health by keeping certain bacteria in check.
   - **Sources**: Sun exposure allows the skin to make vitamin D. Food sources include fatty fish (salmon, sardines), fortified dairy, and egg yolks.
   - **Notes for Women**: Women with low vitamin D may face more frequent digestive issues or notice bone problems over time. Because the sun is not always a reliable source (due to climate or sunscreen use), checking vitamin D levels might be helpful, especially if you have ongoing gut problems.

5. **Vitamin E**
   - **Uses**: Functions as an antioxidant that protects cell membranes.
   - **Sources**: Nuts, seeds, avocados, and vegetable oils.
   - **Notes for Women**: While vitamin E is not as directly linked to gut function as vitamin D or B vitamins, it helps reduce oxidative stress, which can harm tissues over time.

7.3 Important Minerals for Digestive Support

1. **Iron**
   - **Uses**: Needed to make hemoglobin, which carries oxygen in the blood. Adequate oxygen is critical for healthy gut cells.
   - **Sources**: Red meat, poultry, beans, lentils, spinach, and fortified cereals.
   - **Notes for Women**: Women lose iron during menstruation. If iron is low, fatigue and gut sluggishness can occur.

However, taking iron supplements can cause constipation, so finding a comfortable balance is key.

2. **Calcium**
    - **Uses**: Builds and maintains bones and teeth. Also helps with muscle contraction, which includes the muscles in the intestines.
    - **Sources**: Dairy products, tofu, leafy greens, and fortified plant milks.
    - **Notes for Women**: Calcium is often linked to bone health, but it also helps keep smooth muscle working well. When levels are too low, muscle contractions may not be as effective, which can influence how quickly or slowly food moves through the gut.
3. **Magnesium**
    - **Uses**: Supports hundreds of chemical reactions in the body, including muscle relaxation and nerve function. It can help prevent constipation by keeping bowel movements regular.
    - **Sources**: Nuts, seeds, whole grains, dark chocolate, and green leafy vegetables.
    - **Notes for Women**: Magnesium can be helpful around menstruation to reduce cramps. It also can promote better sleep, which is important for gut healing.
4. **Zinc**
    - **Uses**: Aids in tissue repair and supports immune defense. It also helps maintain the gut lining and can reduce the chance of harmful bacteria crossing into the bloodstream.
    - **Sources**: Oysters, beef, pumpkin seeds, beans, and nuts.
    - **Notes for Women**: If you notice slow wound healing or frequent colds, you may need more zinc. Be careful not to overdo zinc supplements, since high doses can interfere with copper levels.
5. **Selenium**
    - **Uses**: Works as an antioxidant that helps protect cells. May help with thyroid function, which can indirectly influence digestion.
    - **Sources**: Brazil nuts, seafood, and whole grains.
    - **Notes for Women**: Taking just one or two Brazil nuts a day can often meet selenium needs. However, large amounts can be harmful, so moderation is best.

7.4 Protein and Gut Repair

Protein plays a vital part in repairing the gut lining. The cells in the intestinal lining turn over quickly, which means they die off and get replaced at a fast rate. Without enough protein, the body might struggle to create new cells. This can lead to a thinner gut barrier, allowing unwanted substances to enter the bloodstream.

- **Complete vs. Incomplete Proteins**:
  Complete proteins have all the essential amino acids. Animal-based foods (meat, fish, eggs, dairy) are usually complete. Most plant proteins are incomplete on their own. Combining foods like rice and beans or peanut butter on whole-wheat bread can create a complete amino acid profile.
- **Protein Amount**:
  Many factors affect how much protein a person needs, like age, activity level, and health status. In general, adult women might aim for about 0.8 grams of protein per kilogram of body weight each day. If you weigh 68 kilograms (about 150 pounds), that is around 54 grams of protein a day. However, women who are pregnant, breastfeeding, or very active may need more.
- **Protein Timing**:
  Spreading protein through meals and snacks rather than eating a large amount at once can help the gut process it more smoothly. This may also help keep blood sugar more stable.

7.5 Carbohydrates: More Than Just Energy

Carbohydrates sometimes get a bad reputation. But not all carbs are equal. Complex carbs in whole grains, legumes, and vegetables provide vitamins, minerals, and fiber. This fiber supports the good bacteria in the colon and helps keep stools at a comfortable consistency.

- **Whole Grains**: Oats, brown rice, quinoa, barley, and whole wheat contain fiber and B vitamins that support gut health. They also tend to break down more slowly, helping with blood sugar control.

- **Legumes**: Beans, lentils, and chickpeas are packed with both protein and fiber. They help feed beneficial gut microbes.
- **Fruits and Vegetables**: Fresh produce offers different types of fiber, plus vitamins and antioxidants. Berries, apples, pears, carrots, and broccoli are especially known for supporting digestion.

Avoiding Highly Processed Carbs
White bread, candy, cookies, and sugary drinks may be tasty, but they can upset the gut's balance if eaten in large amounts. These foods often lack fiber and nutrients. They can also feed bacteria that produce gas or cause inflammation.

7.6 Healthy Fats and Gut Function

Unsaturated Fats
These come from sources like avocados, nuts, seeds, and olive oil. They tend to help the body by reducing harmful cholesterol levels and supporting cell membranes. Omega-3 fats from fish like salmon or sardines can reduce inflammation in the gut.

Saturated Fats
Found in butter, red meat, and coconut oil. In moderate amounts, some saturated fat can fit into a balanced diet. But too much saturated fat can inflame the gut and change the makeup of gut bacteria in ways that might not be ideal.

Trans Fats
These are often found in hydrogenated oils, which used to be common in some processed foods. Most health authorities advise avoiding trans fats because they can harm the heart and may promote inflammation.

7.7 Water and Gut Health

It is easy to overlook water when thinking about nutrients, but proper hydration helps the gut in several ways:

1. **Bowel Regularity**:
   Water makes stools softer and easier to pass. Without enough water, constipation can become a problem.
2. **Nutrient Transport**:
   Blood needs adequate fluid to carry nutrients to cells, including those in the gut lining.
3. **Digestive Juices**:
   The stomach and intestines need fluid to produce mucus, enzymes, and bile to break down food.

How Much Water is Enough?
A common guideline is about 8 cups a day (64 ounces), but needs vary. Factors like weather, exercise, pregnancy, or breastfeeding can raise your fluid requirements. Drinking herbal teas, low-sugar juices, or water-rich foods (cucumber, watermelon) can also help.

7.8 Fiber: The Special Carbohydrate

Fiber deserves extra attention because it is key for gut health. It adds bulk to stools, feeds beneficial bacteria, and helps reduce spikes in blood sugar.

Two Main Kinds of Fiber

1. **Soluble Fiber**
   - Dissolves in water to form a gel-like material.
   - Found in oats, beans, apples, citrus fruits, and carrots.
   - Helps lower cholesterol and can make you feel full longer.
2. **Insoluble Fiber**
   - Does not dissolve in water.
   - Found in whole wheat, brown rice, cauliflower, and potatoes.
   - Speeds the passage of food through the stomach and intestines, which can prevent constipation.

Balancing Fiber
Some women feel bloated if they suddenly increase their fiber intake. It is best to add high-fiber foods gradually and drink more water at the same

time. Over time, the gut adapts to the added fiber, and bloating often goes down.

7.9 Lesser-Known Nutrients for Gut Comfort

1. **L-Glutamine**
    - An amino acid that may help heal the intestinal lining.
    - Found in foods like beef, chicken, fish, dairy, beans, and some leafy vegetables.
    - Certain people with gut issues take L-glutamine supplements, but it is wise to speak with a healthcare professional before adding them.
2. **Choline**
    - Involved in building cell membranes and sending signals in the brain.
    - Sources include eggs, beef liver, chicken, soybeans, and kidney beans.
    - There is some evidence that having enough choline supports overall gut function, especially since it helps maintain strong cells.
3. **Short-Chain Fatty Acids (SCFAs)**
    - Not exactly a nutrient we eat, but rather something produced when good bacteria ferment certain fibers in the colon.
    - SCFAs help keep the colon cells healthy and reduce inflammation.
    - Getting enough resistant starch (found in cooled cooked potatoes, green bananas, or cooked then cooled rice) can boost SCFA production.

7.10 Nutrient Timing and Meal Planning

Eating Smaller, Balanced Meals

Large meals can strain the digestive system, especially if they are high in fat or sugar. Spreading out nutrients throughout the day may help the gut cope better. For example, rather than one big lunch, you might eat a moderate lunch and have a nutritious snack a few hours later.

Combining Macronutrients
Pairing carbohydrates with protein and healthy fats can slow the release of sugar into the bloodstream and support stable energy levels. An example is having whole-grain toast (complex carbs) with peanut butter (healthy fats and some protein).

Variety is Key
Eating the same meals every day can limit the range of nutrients and types of fiber you get. Try to add different fruits, vegetables, proteins, and grains to cover various vitamins and minerals.

7.11 Special Times When Nutrients Matter Even More

1. **Pregnancy**
     - The body's demand for protein, iron, folate, and other nutrients rises.
     - Folate (vitamin B9) is very important in preventing birth defects.
     - Extra iron is often needed to support the increased blood volume.
2. **Menopause**
     - Changes in hormone levels can affect how the gut functions.
     - Calcium and vitamin D become more crucial for bone health, and that also helps with muscle function in the gut.
     - Some women find that adjusting fiber intake can help with constipation that may appear during this stage.
3. **Post-Surgery or Illness**
     - The gut might need more protein for tissue repair.
     - Vitamins and minerals are needed to help the immune system get back on track.

7.12 Reducing Toxins That Interfere with Nutrient Use

While focusing on nutrients is important, it is also useful to look at what might block their absorption. Certain toxins or chemicals in foods can reduce the body's ability to take in vitamins and minerals.

- **Pesticides**: Some chemicals used to treat crops might interfere with gut bacteria or cause inflammation. Washing produce thoroughly or choosing organic when possible can help.
- **Additives and Preservatives**: These can irritate the lining of the gut in some individuals, making nutrient absorption harder.
- **Excess Alcohol**: Drinking too much can damage cells in the stomach and intestines, and it can reduce levels of certain B vitamins.

7.13 Supplements: When and How

While a balanced diet is the best way to get nutrients, some women may need supplements:

- **Multivitamins**: Can fill in gaps for those with restricted diets.
- **Vitamin D and Calcium**: Often suggested for women who do not get enough from sunlight and food.
- **Iron**: May be needed if tests show anemia or low iron stores.
- **Magnesium**: Some women find it helps with bowel regularity or muscle cramps.

Before starting supplements, it can be helpful to have a blood test and speak to a healthcare provider. Taking too much of certain nutrients can lead to issues like toxicity or imbalances that affect how the body absorbs other vitamins and minerals.

7.14 Putting Knowledge Into Action

- **Sample Breakfast**: Oatmeal topped with berries and a spoonful of nut butter. This gives soluble fiber, antioxidants, healthy fats, and some protein.
- **Sample Lunch**: Salad with leafy greens, grilled chicken or beans, chopped vegetables, and a whole-grain roll. The greens offer vitamin K and magnesium, while the chicken or beans supply protein and nutrients like B vitamins.
- **Sample Dinner**: Salmon (for omega-3 fats) with quinoa and steamed broccoli. Quinoa provides complex carbs and magnesium, while broccoli has fiber, vitamin C, and other minerals.
- **Snacks**: Fruits, yogurt, nuts, or seeds can provide extra nutrients without overwhelming the gut.

By choosing meals that mix different food groups, you boost your chance of getting a wide range of nutrients. Over time, these small steps can add up to better gut health.

7.15 Spotting Early Signs of Nutrient Deficiency

- **Chronic Fatigue**: Could point to low iron, low B12, or general malnutrition.
- **Brittle Hair and Nails**: Sometimes linked to low protein, low iron, or low zinc.
- **Frequent Illnesses**: Might be a sign of low vitamin C, low zinc, or poor overall diet.
- **Skin Issues**: Acne or rashes can have many causes, but in some cases, they relate to low vitamin A, vitamin E, or essential fatty acids.

If these signs appear, it might be wise to review your eating habits and check nutrient levels through blood tests.

7.16 Myths About Diet and Gut Health

- **Myth**: Fat-free diets are always best.
  - **Truth**: The body needs healthy fats for cell membranes, hormone production, and nutrient absorption.
- **Myth**: High-protein, low-carb diets are the only way to lose weight.
  - **Truth**: While protein is important, the gut also needs carbohydrates, especially fiber, for healthy bacterial balance and bowel function.
- **Myth**: If a supplement label says "natural," it must be safe.
  - **Truth**: The term "natural" is not well regulated. Always check with a professional before taking large doses of any supplement.

7.17 Balancing Meals During Stress

When under stress, some women reach for comfort foods that might be high in sugar or unhealthy fats. While an occasional treat is fine, it is wise to create stress-coping strategies that do not always center on food. Simple things like a warm herbal tea or a calming walk can help reduce tension without overwhelming the gut.

7.18 Long-Term Goals for Nutrient Intake

1. **Aim for Consistency**
   Rather than jumping from one diet trend to another, build a balanced eating pattern that you can keep up over time.
2. **Check Your Levels Periodically**
   If you have ongoing digestive issues or suspect a deficiency, regular blood tests can confirm whether your plan is working.
3. **Stay Flexible**
   Your nutrient needs can change. Pregnancy, aging, new health conditions, or a sudden increase in physical activity might call for adjustments.

4. **Listen to Your Body**
   Pay attention to how you feel after certain meals. If you notice bloating, low energy, or discomfort, see if certain nutrients might be missing or excessive.

7.19 Common Pitfalls

- **Over-Reliance on Processed Snacks**: Even if they claim to have added vitamins, they often contain a lot of sugar, salt, and additives that can upset the gut.
- **Skipping Meals**: This can lead to nutrient gaps and unsteady energy levels.
- **Focusing on One Nutrient**: For instance, loading up only on calcium while ignoring magnesium, vitamin D, and other co-factors can cause imbalances.
- **Ignoring Label Reading**: Some "health" products might have hidden chemicals or too much sugar, so reading labels is helpful.

7.20 Conclusion to Chapter 7

Nutrients are the building blocks that keep our guts running smoothly. Proteins, carbs, fats, vitamins, and minerals all have roles in digestion, from helping repair the gut lining to fueling beneficial bacteria. Women can have different needs based on life stages and hormone fluctuations. By aiming for a balanced diet filled with whole foods, it is possible to support both digestive comfort and overall wellbeing.

In the next chapter, we will focus on prebiotics and probiotics, which are special parts of food and supplements that can support or add healthy bacteria to the gut. Building on what you have learned here about basic nutrients, you will see how directing more care toward specific elements of the diet can give your gut an extra boost.

Chapter 8

Prebiotics and Probiotics

Prebiotics and probiotics have gained attention in recent years as people search for ways to improve gut health. Although they sound similar, they serve different functions. Prebiotics feed the helpful bacteria already in the gut, while probiotics add new beneficial microbes. In this chapter, we will look at how they work, why they matter for women, and how to include them in daily life.

8.1 Defining Prebiotics and Probiotics

Prebiotics

- **What They Are**: Nondigestible fibers or other substances that boost the growth of helpful bacteria in the gut.
- **Examples**: Inulin, fructooligosaccharides (FOS), galactooligosaccharides (GOS), and resistant starches. These can be found in foods like chicory root, onions, garlic, bananas, and whole grains.

Probiotics

- **What They Are**: Live microorganisms that, when taken in the right amounts, can improve the balance of gut bacteria.
- **Examples**: Certain strains of Lactobacillus, Bifidobacterium, and Saccharomyces. These are found in fermented foods like yogurt, kefir, sauerkraut, kimchi, and some cheeses, as well as dietary supplements.

8.2 How Prebiotics Work

Prebiotics act as food for the beneficial bacteria that live in the large intestine. Since the human body cannot fully break down certain fibers or starches, these substances pass into the colon. There, bacteria ferment them, producing short-chain fatty acids (SCFAs) and other compounds that keep the colon cells healthy. This process can reduce inflammation, support nutrient absorption, and strengthen the gut barrier.

Benefits of Prebiotics for Women

- **Hormone Support**: By feeding the right bacteria, prebiotics may help with the breakdown of certain hormones or their byproducts, reducing issues like bloating or mood swings.
- **Weight Control**: Some prebiotics can make you feel full longer, which might help manage weight.
- **Better Mineral Absorption**: SCFAs produced by fermentation can enhance the absorption of minerals like calcium and magnesium, which is useful for women's bone health.

8.3 How Probiotics Work

Probiotics add live bacteria to the digestive tract. If they survive stomach acid and reach the colon, they can settle in or at least provide benefits while passing through. These bacteria can:

- Compete with harmful microbes for space and nutrients.
- Produce compounds that lower the gut's pH, making it harder for harmful bacteria to grow.
- Signal the immune system to function more efficiently.

Benefits of Probiotics for Women

- **Vaginal Health**: Certain probiotic strains may help maintain a healthy vaginal environment, reducing the risk of yeast or urinary tract infections.
- **Mood and Stress**: Some strains produce chemicals linked to calmer moods.
- **Digestion and Regularity**: People with constipation or diarrhea may find relief when adding specific probiotic strains to their diet.

8.4 Sources of Prebiotics

1. **Chicory Root**
   - Often added to foods or coffee substitutes for its inulin content.
   - Can cause gas or bloating in large amounts if the gut is not used to it.
2. **Onions and Garlic**
   - Contain inulin and fructooligosaccharides.
   - Also add flavor to meals.
   - Cooking them can make them easier on the stomach for some individuals.
3. **Bananas**
   - Green (less ripe) bananas have more resistant starch, a type of prebiotic.
   - Adding sliced banana to yogurt can give a double benefit of prebiotic plus probiotic.
4. **Whole Grains**
   - Oats, wheat, barley, and rye contain fibers and other prebiotic compounds.
   - Look for minimally processed options to get the full benefit.
5. **Beans and Legumes**
   - Rich in soluble fiber and resistant starch.
   - Black beans, lentils, chickpeas, and kidney beans can feed good gut bacteria.

8.5 Sources of Probiotics

1. **Yogurt**
   - One of the most common probiotic foods.
   - Check labels for "live and active cultures."
   - Some brands add too much sugar, so reading the nutrition facts is helpful.
2. **Kefir**
   - A fermented milk drink that has a variety of bacterial strains, sometimes more than yogurt.

- Tangy taste and can be used in smoothies or consumed plain.
3. **Sauerkraut and Kimchi**
    - Fermented cabbage dishes.
    - Kimchi often includes spices, garlic, and other vegetables, adding extra nutrients.
    - Must be unpasteurized if you want live bacteria. Heat can kill the helpful microbes.
4. **Kombucha**
    - Fermented tea that contains bacteria and yeast.
    - Sometimes has a slight fizz and a sour taste.
    - Look for low-sugar varieties to avoid feeding harmful bacteria with excess sugar.
5. **Fermented Vegetables and Pickles**
    - Carrots, beets, cucumbers, and other vegetables can be fermented at home or purchased from stores.
    - As with sauerkraut, they need to be unpasteurized to retain beneficial bacteria.
6. **Probiotic Supplements**
    - Available in pills, powders, or liquids.
    - Come in different strains and strengths.
    - It is smart to choose a product that lists specific strains and an expiration date.

8.6 Choosing the Right Strains

Not all probiotic strains are the same. Some are best for general digestive health, while others target specific issues:

- **Lactobacillus rhamnosus GG**: Known for supporting overall gut health and might help reduce diarrhea.
- **Bifidobacterium longum**: May help reduce stress-related gut symptoms and support regularity.
- **Saccharomyces boulardii**: A yeast-based probiotic often used to address traveler's diarrhea or antibiotic-associated diarrhea.
- **Lactobacillus acidophilus**: Common in yogurt and can support vaginal health.

Women who want a targeted benefit, such as relief from constipation or help with vaginal health, might look for a product designed for that purpose. Reading labels and researching strains can make a difference in choosing the right probiotic.

8.7 Balancing Prebiotics and Probiotics

Why Both Matter
Prebiotics and probiotics work hand in hand. If you add helpful bacteria but do not feed them properly (through fiber-rich foods), they may not thrive. Meanwhile, if you eat plenty of prebiotics but lack diverse good bacteria, you might not get the full benefit of fermentation.

How to Combine Them

- Start your day with a probiotic food like yogurt or kefir, and include a source of prebiotics, such as a banana or some oats.
- Have a lunch or dinner that includes both cooked beans (prebiotic) and a side of sauerkraut (probiotic).

Over time, this regular combination can help establish and maintain a balanced gut community.

8.8 Understanding Synbiotics

A "synbiotic" is a product that contains both prebiotics and probiotics. The idea is to deliver beneficial bacteria along with the food they need to grow. Some synbiotic supplements are on the market, and certain foods may also be formulated this way. For example, a yogurt might have extra inulin added to it. Reading labels is key if you are looking for a synbiotic product.

8.9 Women's Health Issues and Probiotics

1. **Urinary Tract and Vaginal Infections**
    - Some probiotic strains can lower the growth of harmful bacteria or yeast in the genital area.
    - Taking these strains may help women who get frequent urinary or yeast infections.
2. **Stress and Mood**
    - Certain probiotics help produce or regulate neurotransmitters in the gut, which can improve mood.
    - Women who face stress-related digestive problems might see benefits from adding these strains to their daily routine.
3. **Weight Control**
    - While probiotics alone will not cause weight loss, they can support a healthy metabolism by keeping gut bacteria balanced.
    - This balance might make it easier to manage cravings or maintain stable energy levels.

8.10 When Prebiotics or Probiotics Might Cause Discomfort

Bloating and Gas
Sometimes, adding high amounts of prebiotics (like inulin) too quickly can trigger bloating or gas. This can happen if the gut bacteria ferment the fiber faster than your body is used to handling. Gradual increases in fiber intake can help.

Temporary Upset
Probiotic foods can sometimes cause loose stools or mild cramping when first introduced, especially if you consume more than your gut is ready for. This usually settles down over time. If it continues, it might be worth trying a different probiotic strain or smaller doses.

Allergic Reactions
Rarely, a person may have an allergic reaction to a specific probiotic. For example, if you are allergic to dairy, you might have problems with

yogurt-based probiotics. Always check ingredients if you have known food allergies.

8.11 Practical Tips for Adding Prebiotics

1. **Go Slowly**
   If your current diet is low in fiber, add one new prebiotic-rich food at a time. For example, add half a cup of beans or a small portion of oats to see how you react.
2. **Mix Different Foods**
   Variety helps feed different strains of bacteria. Try onions in a stir-fry, bananas in a smoothie, and whole-grain bread for a sandwich.
3. **Cook or Choose Carefully**
   Cooked onions may be gentler on the stomach than raw onions. Green bananas might be too starchy for some; letting them ripen a bit can reduce the resistant starch.

8.12 Practical Tips for Adding Probiotics

1. **Check Labels**
   Make sure the product states it has live and active cultures. If it is pasteurized after fermentation, many of the beneficial microbes may be gone.
2. **Refrigeration**
   Some probiotic foods and supplements need to be kept cold to stay alive. Keep them in the fridge if recommended.
3. **Mind the Sugar**
   Many yogurt products have added sweeteners. Too much sugar can encourage less desirable bacteria. Choosing plain or low-sugar options is often better.
4. **Different Strains**
   Some women experiment with various probiotic strains to see which works best. If a product or brand does not give you results after a month or so, consider trying another strain or approach.

8.13 Probiotics and Antibiotics

Antibiotics can wipe out a lot of bacteria in your body, both harmful and beneficial. This can disrupt the gut ecosystem, sometimes causing diarrhea or yeast overgrowth. Taking a probiotic, either during or after antibiotic therapy, can help rebuild a healthy balance. However, it is often advised to take the probiotic a few hours away from the antibiotic to reduce the chance of killing the beneficial microbes.

8.14 Homemade Fermentation

Some women decide to ferment foods at home, such as making yogurt, kefir, or fermented vegetables. This can be more cost-effective and lets you control what goes into the final product. However, it is crucial to use safe practices:

- Clean jars and utensils thoroughly.
- Follow reliable recipes.
- Watch out for signs of mold or off smells.
- Store fermented items at the right temperature.

Homemade fermentation can be fun, but safety should come first to avoid harmful bacteria.

8.15 The Influence of Diet and Lifestyle on Probiotic Effectiveness

Even if you eat probiotics, an overall unhealthy diet can prevent them from helping as much as they could. Eating a lot of sugar or highly processed foods can increase harmful bacteria, making it harder for the probiotics to settle in. Likewise, chronic stress, poor sleep, and lack of exercise can weaken the gut environment. So, it is wise to view probiotics as part of a larger plan that includes balanced meals, hydration, and good sleep.

8.16 Special Considerations for Certain Life Stages

1. **Pregnancy**
    - Some probiotics can help reduce constipation or the risk of certain infections.
    - Always talk with a healthcare professional before starting any supplement.
2. **Breastfeeding**
    - A mother's gut health can affect her milk and her energy levels. Probiotics might help reduce the chance of digestive issues.
    - However, checking with a doctor is a good idea to ensure safety for both mother and baby.
3. **Menopause**
    - Hormone changes can alter gut bacteria. Probiotics may help ease digestive shifts and maintain bowel regularity.

8.17 Are All Supplements Equal?

Not all probiotic supplements deliver what they promise. Some have low counts of live bacteria by the time they reach store shelves. Others might not list the strains clearly. Before investing in a probiotic supplement, look for:

- A brand that specifies strain types and amounts (measured in CFUs, or colony-forming units).
- An expiration date or "best by" date.
- Storage instructions (some need refrigeration).
- Third-party testing or certification if possible.

If you are unsure, ask a pharmacist or health professional for guidance.

8.18 Could You Have Too Much?

Generally, eating foods with prebiotics and probiotics is safe. However, very high amounts of fiber or certain probiotic strains can cause bloating, cramping, or diarrhea in some people. Moderation is important. If you notice discomfort, reduce your intake for a while, then try adding these foods or supplements back in small amounts.

8.19 Research and Future Directions

Scientists continue to study specific strains of bacteria to see how they might help with issues like anxiety, obesity, or autoimmune conditions. Some ongoing areas of research include:

1. **Psychobiotics**: Probiotics that might improve mental health by producing chemicals that reduce stress or support a stable mood.
2. **Personalized Strains**: In the future, people might have personalized probiotic blends based on their gut microbiome profile.
3. **Quality Control**: Efforts are being made to regulate the probiotic industry so that products actually contain what the labels promise.

8.20 Conclusion to Chapter 8

Prebiotics and probiotics are like partners in supporting a healthy gut. Prebiotics feed your existing beneficial bacteria, while probiotics add new ones to the mix. When chosen wisely, they can help with digestion, immunity, and even stress management. Women may find these especially helpful for issues related to hormone changes, urinary health, and mood.

In the next chapters, we will discuss more about fiber and rest, including how simple daily routines can give your gut a break and support better digestion. Building on what you have learned about prebiotics and probiotics, you will see how each part of a balanced lifestyle can work together to keep your gut environment in good shape.

Chapter 9

Fiber and Helpful Bacteria

Fiber is not just about regular bowel movements. It also feeds the helpful bacteria in the gut and affects many parts of a woman's wellbeing. Some women assume fiber is dull or only linked to preventing constipation. In truth, fiber can support energy levels, help with weight balance, and aid in hormone management. It can even reduce certain risks over time. In this chapter, we will look at different types of fiber, how fiber feeds bacteria in the gut, and why this matters for women. We will also cover practical ways to include more fiber without upsetting the stomach.

9.1 Introduction to Fiber

Fiber is a form of carbohydrate that our bodies cannot fully break down. This means it moves through the gut in ways other carbohydrates cannot. Because fiber passes through the intestines mostly intact, it helps with stool formation, feeds bacteria, and keeps the gut active.

Women often deal with hormone changes and stress factors that may cause issues like bloating or constipation. Fiber can help manage these concerns by promoting a stable environment in the gut. It also has the power to slow the release of sugar into the blood, which can help keep energy levels steady.

Fiber is found in many foods, such as fruits, vegetables, beans, lentils, nuts, seeds, and whole grains. Different types of fiber serve different roles, but overall, they help promote variety in the gut's microbial population. This varied microbial population can be a protective factor against certain health problems.

9.2 Why Fiber is Special for Women

Women have times in life when hormone levels surge or dip, such as during monthly cycles, pregnancy, and menopause. Hormones can affect gut movement and water balance in the body. For instance, some women notice bloating or constipation before a menstrual cycle. Fiber helps by moving waste through more smoothly, reducing some of that tension.

Fiber can also help support stable blood sugar levels. Women who struggle with mood issues related to changes in blood sugar might find relief in a consistent intake of high-fiber foods. Fiber leads to a steadier supply of energy, instead of rapid sugar spikes that may affect mood or energy.

Furthermore, certain types of fiber can bind to extra estrogen in the intestines, helping the body remove it. For women who have issues linked to high estrogen, this may be helpful. While fiber alone will not solve hormone imbalance, it can be part of a balanced plan.

9.3 Types of Fiber: Soluble and Insoluble

Fiber is usually sorted into two main types: soluble and insoluble. Both types are important, but they have different jobs in the gut.

1. **Soluble Fiber**
    - Dissolves in water to create a gel-like substance.
    - Slows digestion, which can help the body absorb nutrients at a steady pace.
    - May help lower cholesterol by binding to it in the gut.
    - Found in oats, beans, lentils, apples, carrots, and citrus fruits.
2. **Insoluble Fiber**
    - Does not dissolve in water.
    - Adds bulk to stool and can help things move along in the colon.
    - Often recommended to help with constipation.
    - Found in whole wheat flour, wheat bran, nuts, beans, cauliflower, and potatoes with skins.

Some foods have both soluble and insoluble fiber. For instance, an apple with the skin has insoluble fiber in the peel and soluble fiber in the flesh. Eating a variety of whole plant foods is the best way to cover both categories.

9.4 Resistant Starch: A Special Kind of Fiber

Resistant starch acts like fiber even though it is technically a starch. The body finds it tough to break down, so it travels to the large intestine mostly intact. There, it can be fermented by helpful bacteria, producing compounds that support the gut lining.

Foods that contain resistant starch include green bananas, cooked and cooled potatoes or rice, and certain legumes. When these foods are cooked and then allowed to cool, some of the starch becomes "resistant," meaning it resists digestion in the small intestine. This leads to more fermentation in the colon.

Women who want to ease into resistant starch can start by adding a small serving of cooled rice or a half green banana. Jumping into large amounts may cause extra gas or bloating if the gut is not used to it. Over time, as the gut adapts, these side effects often lessen.

9.5 The Helpful Bacteria in Our Gut

The gut hosts trillions of bacteria. Many are helpful because they break down parts of food the body cannot digest. They also make substances that can be useful for the colon walls, the immune system, and even the brain. But these microbes need the right food. That is where fiber steps in.

When these helpful bacteria feed on fiber, they multiply. This growth can make it harder for harmful bacteria to take over. Also, the byproducts of fiber fermentation can lower the pH in parts of the colon. A lower pH can discourage some harmful bacteria from thriving.

Women's bacterial communities may shift due to hormonal changes or life events like pregnancy, antibiotic use, or shifts in diet. Eating enough fiber can help keep the bacterial community varied and strong, which might support better mood stability and more predictable digestion.

9.6 How Fiber Feeds Good Bacteria

When a person eats fiber, it is not fully broken down in the stomach or small intestine. As the fiber reaches the large intestine, bacteria latch onto it and begin to ferment it. Fermentation breaks the fiber into smaller compounds like short-chain fatty acids (SCFAs).

Some of the main SCFAs are acetate, propionate, and butyrate. Butyrate is often studied because it can help keep the cells in the colon healthy. Healthy colon cells can form a tighter barrier, blocking harmful substances from entering the bloodstream.

Women who want to support these good bacteria can eat foods like onions, garlic, oats, beans, and artichokes. Varied sources of fiber often lead to a more diverse bacterial population. That variety, in turn, can give better protection against harmful microbes.

9.7 Fiber Fermentation and Short-Chain Fatty Acids

SCFAs are important because they support the mucus layer in the gut. This layer is like a cushion that protects the gut lining from direct contact with unwanted items. A strong mucus layer can reduce irritation and may lessen the risk of leaky gut.

Some SCFAs can also travel through the bloodstream. This means they can influence other parts of the body, possibly affecting how the liver, brain, or immune cells function. These effects are still being studied, but they show how fiber and gut bacteria can have a wide-ranging influence.

For women, stable SCFA levels might help maintain calm digestion and balanced immune responses. While SCFAs alone are not a cure for hormonal or mood issues, they appear to be part of the overall set of factors that keep the body balanced.

9.8 Health Gains Linked to SCFA Production

1. **Reduced Inflammation**: SCFAs can signal the immune system to avoid overreacting. Low-grade inflammation is linked to many long-term health problems, so keeping inflammation at bay is helpful.
2. **Better Blood Sugar Control**: Some research suggests that certain SCFAs may help the body use insulin more effectively. This could be important for women who face insulin resistance or polycystic ovary syndrome (PCOS).
3. **Improved Colon Health**: Butyrate can fuel colon cells, helping them repair and renew. This can help reduce the chance of long-term colon problems.
4. **Support for Weight Balance**: While fiber alone is not a magic fix, it may help reduce overeating by promoting fullness. SCFAs produced from fiber fermentation can also play a part in signaling the brain about satiety.

9.9 Meeting Fiber Goals

Most health guidelines suggest that adult women get about 25 to 30 grams of fiber per day, though some experts believe women could benefit from even more, depending on their age and overall health. However, many women do not reach these amounts.

The reasons vary. Some rely on fast foods or processed meals low in fiber. Others are unsure which foods contain fiber or worry about bloating. Still, adding more fiber does not need to be complicated. Simple steps, such as swapping white bread for whole wheat bread or having an apple instead of juice, can add up over time.

9.10 Good Sources of Fiber

- **Beans and Lentils**: Black beans, kidney beans, chickpeas, and lentils are high in fiber. They also have protein and other nutrients.
- **Whole Grains**: Oats, brown rice, bulgur, quinoa, and whole wheat pasta can help you reach fiber goals.
- **Fruits**: Apples, pears, berries, oranges, and bananas have fiber, especially if you keep the edible skin on apples and pears.
- **Vegetables**: Broccoli, Brussels sprouts, carrots, sweet potatoes (with skins), and peas.
- **Seeds and Nuts**: Chia seeds, flaxseeds, almonds, pistachios, and walnuts.

A balanced approach might include beans a few days a week, whole grains at least once or twice a day, and several servings of fruits and vegetables throughout each day.

9.11 Minimizing Gas and Bloating

Some women worry that high-fiber foods cause gas or bloating. While this can happen, there are ways to reduce discomfort:

1. **Increase Slowly**: Do not double or triple your fiber intake overnight. Add a small amount, like a half-cup of beans or a tablespoon of flaxseeds, and watch how your body reacts.
2. **Stay Hydrated**: Fiber swells and moves better through the gut if there is enough water. Low fluid intake can make high-fiber foods harder to pass.
3. **Try Soaking and Rinsing**: If beans or lentils cause discomfort, soaking them overnight and rinsing them well before cooking can help remove some of the compounds that cause gas.
4. **Cook Your Veggies**: Raw vegetables can be harder to handle than cooked ones. Steaming or roasting can make the fiber easier to process.

9.12 Tips to Add More Fiber

- **Swap White for Brown**: Choose brown rice, whole wheat bread, or whole wheat pasta in place of white varieties.
- **Snack on Whole Fruits**: Instead of fruit juice, eat the whole fruit to gain fiber.
- **Stir Seeds into Meals**: Add chia seeds or ground flaxseeds to cereal, yogurt, or smoothies.
- **Use Lentils in Soups**: Lentils cook quickly and add both fiber and protein to dishes.
- **Make Veggies a Main Dish**: Plan meals around vegetables instead of thinking of them as side dishes. A hearty vegetable stew can offer high amounts of fiber.

If you aim for small changes, you might see a difference in digestion without feeling overwhelmed. Over time, fiber-rich eating can become a normal part of daily life.

9.13 Fiber's Link to Weight Management

Eating more fiber can help promote a sense of fullness after meals, which may reduce the urge to snack on sugary or fatty foods. This can be an asset for women who want to stay at a healthy weight or reduce weight. Fiber-rich foods often have fewer calories per serving compared to processed foods, allowing for bigger portions that still help with overall calorie balance.

Research shows that people who regularly eat high-fiber diets often have better control over hunger signals. Since many women experience cravings linked to stress or hormone changes, fiber might help by leveling blood sugar swings. This does not mean fiber automatically leads to weight loss. Rather, it can be an extra tool that supports a balanced approach to eating.

9.14 Fiber for Different Life Stages

1. **Teen Years**: Young women who are growing can benefit from fiber to help regulate hormones and support bone health. A diet that includes whole grains, fruits, and vegetables can build lasting habits.
2. **Pregnancy**: Bowel movements can slow during pregnancy. Fiber can relieve constipation and may help stabilize blood sugar. Expectant mothers should also drink enough water to move fiber along.
3. **Menopause**: Hormone changes can lead to shifts in how the body stores fat or handles water. Fiber can help control cholesterol, weight, and digestive comfort during these years.

At each stage, the basic idea stays the same: aim for varied, whole foods that provide both soluble and insoluble fiber.

9.15 Real World Examples

- **Maria's Lunch Makeover**: Maria used to eat a white bread sandwich with processed meat and a bag of chips. When she switched to a whole wheat wrap filled with chickpeas, spinach, tomato, and avocado, she noticed less bloating and more energy. By the afternoon, she did not feel as tired.
- **Jenna's Weekend Cooking**: Jenna started batch-cooking a big pot of lentil soup each weekend. She found this helped her and her family eat fiber-rich meals for multiple lunches. Over a few months, she said her bowel movements became more regular.
- **Ava's Smoothie Boost**: Ava began adding a tablespoon of ground flaxseeds to her morning smoothie. She used berries, spinach, almond milk, and a little yogurt. This small step helped her feel fuller until lunchtime.

9.16 Myths about Fiber

1. **Myth**: Fiber is only for older people with constipation.
   Truth: Fiber benefits all ages by supporting healthy digestion, blood sugar, and bacteria balance.
2. **Myth**: A fiber supplement is enough.
   Truth: While supplements can help, real foods also supply vitamins, minerals, and other compounds that support health in ways supplements cannot.
3. **Myth**: All fiber is the same.
   Truth: Different fibers have different effects. Eating a range of high-fiber foods helps you gain diverse benefits.

9.17 Summary: Fiber's Big Impact

Fiber is more than a tool for going to the bathroom. It nourishes the helpful bacteria in the gut, supports stable blood sugar, helps manage appetite, and possibly assists in hormone balance. Women can face extra challenges because of monthly cycles, pregnancy, and menopause, but a fiber-rich diet can support them at every step. By including a mix of whole grains, legumes, fruits, vegetables, nuts, and seeds, women can move closer to a gut environment that feels balanced and strong.

9.18 Conclusion to Chapter 9

Fiber is a strong ally for women's digestion and overall wellbeing. It works by feeding beneficial bacteria, contributing to gut barrier health, and helping regulate the pace of digestion. Although some women worry about bloating, introducing fiber slowly and pairing it with enough fluids can often help the body adjust.

In the next chapter, we will cover rest and routine. We will see how daily habits, such as regular sleep and consistent meal times, can help the gut. These strategies, combined with the right food choices, can help women feel more at ease both physically and mentally.

Chapter 10

Rest and Routine

Modern life can be busy and packed with responsibilities. Women often juggle family duties, career demands, social events, and personal goals. In the middle of this, rest might seem like a luxury rather than a necessity. However, restful sleep and stable daily routines can support a healthy gut and mind. In this chapter, we will look at why rest matters, how daily structure affects digestion, and ways to form habits that support a calmer body.

10.1 Why Rest Matters for Digestion

Digestion does not just happen when we eat. It continues as food moves through the stomach, intestines, and colon. When we are asleep or relaxed, the body can focus on these internal processes. Blood flow shifts to the digestive tract, and cells can repair and renew. Without enough rest, this process can be disrupted, leading to issues like indigestion or less effective nutrient uptake.

Women might struggle more with rest if they have an uneven schedule or if hormone changes affect their sleep patterns. For example, some women have trouble sleeping before a menstrual cycle. Others might find that pregnancy disrupts sleep due to frequent trips to the bathroom or discomfort. Still, aiming for enough rest is key to helping the gut function smoothly.

10.2 The Body's Internal Clock

The body runs on a "clock" known as the circadian rhythm. This rhythm guides when we feel awake or tired and also impacts hormone release, metabolism, and digestion. When the circadian rhythm is stable, we feel more alert in the morning and sleepy at night. The gut also works more effectively when it follows a pattern.

Shifting bedtimes or eating times can confuse the gut. People who work night shifts often face higher risks of digestive problems because their gut is constantly trying to adjust. Even smaller changes, like staying up too late or skipping meals, can throw off the gut's schedule. For women who already have hormone swings, maintaining a stable circadian rhythm can help reduce extra stress on the body.

10.3 The Link Between Sleep and Hunger Hormones

Two hormones play a large part in controlling hunger: ghrelin and leptin. Ghrelin is often called the "hunger hormone" because it encourages us to eat, while leptin signals when we feel full. Lack of sleep can raise ghrelin levels and reduce leptin, leading to stronger hunger signals and possible overeating.

Women who are tired may crave sugary or fatty foods to get quick energy. Over time, these cravings can lead to unbalanced meals and gut issues, especially if processed snacks replace fiber-rich foods. By getting enough quality sleep, women can help keep hunger hormones and gut bacteria more stable, lowering the chance of constant cravings.

10.4 Building a Consistent Sleep Schedule

1. **Choose a Bedtime and Stick to It**: Going to bed at the same time each night helps the body anticipate sleep. This might reduce the time it takes to drift off.
2. **Create a Calm Environment**: Dim lights, a cooler room temperature, and limited noise can make it easier to rest. Some women use earplugs or masks if they live in loud or bright places.
3. **Limit Screens**: The blue light from phones, computers, or TVs can confuse the brain into thinking it is daytime. Reducing screen use at least 30 minutes before bedtime may help.
4. **Avoid Heavy Meals Late at Night**: Digestion can disrupt sleep if the stomach is too busy breaking down a large meal. A small, light snack is generally better if you need to eat close to bedtime.

A steady sleep schedule can pay off for gut health, reducing episodes of indigestion or irregular bowel movements.

10.5 Creating a Daily Routine for Digestion

1. **Regular Meal Times**: Eating around the same time each day can help the gut release enzymes and acids on a predictable schedule. Some women find that three meals a day works best, while others prefer smaller, more frequent meals.
2. **Plan Bathroom Breaks**: It might sound odd, but setting aside time for the bathroom in the morning or evening can train the body. Rushed mornings often cause people to ignore the urge to go, which can lead to constipation.
3. **Include Movement**: Gentle exercise, like walking or light stretching, helps food move along through the intestines. Even a short break to walk around every couple of hours can assist digestion.
4. **Stay Hydrated**: Drinking water regularly rather than gulping it all at once can keep the digestive system running smoothly.

10.6 The Power of Naps (But Not Too Long)

Short naps can be refreshing, especially if night-time sleep was cut short. A nap of 20-30 minutes can boost focus and reduce stress hormones, which in turn can help the gut. However, very long naps might disrupt nighttime sleep, creating a vicious cycle.

For women who feel an energy dip midday, a brief nap may reduce the need for excessive coffee or sugary snacks. This can indirectly help the gut by lowering intake of irritants like caffeine or refined sugar. The key is to keep naps short so the body still feels ready for bed later.

10.7 Stress and Sleep Disturbances

Stress can keep the mind racing, making it hard to fall asleep. Women often face a mix of responsibilities that increase stress, from caring for children or older relatives to meeting work deadlines. This stress can lead to a loop: stress makes it hard to sleep, lack of sleep increases stress the next day, and the gut feels the strain.

Breaking the loop can involve setting aside a "wind-down" period before bed. This might mean turning off work notifications, doing a calming activity like reading a light book (not on a bright screen), or practicing simple breathing exercises. Even a short relaxation routine before bed can send signals to the brain that it is time to rest.

10.8 Nighttime Digestive Issues

Heartburn, acid reflux, or indigestion can worsen at night if a person lies down too soon after eating a big meal. Gravity helps keep stomach acid down when we sit or stand, but lying flat can allow it to creep back up into the esophagus.

To reduce nighttime digestive issues:

- Wait at least 2-3 hours after dinner before going to sleep.
- Keep the head of the bed raised a bit, if acid reflux is a major concern.
- Avoid large amounts of spicy or acidic foods close to bedtime.

Women who are pregnant might feel extra pressure on the stomach as the uterus grows, making reflux worse. A careful sleep posture, along with smaller meals, can help.

10.9 Shift Work and Gut Health

Some women work in roles that require shifts at odd hours, such as nurses, factory workers, or customer service representatives in 24-hour settings. Shift work can clash with the normal circadian rhythm. The body might think it is nighttime when you are at work and daytime when you are trying to sleep.

Over time, shift work can lead to digestive chaos, including constipation or frequent trips to the bathroom at odd times. Trying to keep some consistency—like eating similar "meal times" relative to your work schedule—can provide a routine for the gut. Also, making the sleep environment as dark and quiet as possible, even if it is daytime, can help trick the body into resting more deeply.

10.10 Travel and Time Zone Changes

Going across time zones can cause something called "jet lag." This happens when the body's clock is not in sync with local day and night cycles. Besides feeling tired or alert at the wrong times, the gut can also get confused. You may feel hungry at 2 a.m. local time or struggle with constipation.

To adjust faster:

- Try to adapt meal and sleep times to the new time zone as soon as possible.
- Stay hydrated to help the body cope with the stress of travel.
- If the trip is long, allow a day or two before major activities so the body can settle.

Women who travel often for work might benefit from a travel routine, such as carrying fiber-rich snacks and using earplugs or an eye mask to improve rest on planes or in new environments.

10.11 Hormonal Changes and Sleep Quality

Women may have sleep disturbances around their menstrual cycle, in pregnancy, or during menopause. For some, hot flashes or night sweats can make restful sleep hard. Others might feel anxious or moody due to hormone shifts, which keeps them awake.

Some tips for these stages:

- Wear breathable sleepwear and keep the room cool.
- Consider a light blanket or layer system so you can adjust if you get too hot or cold.
- A mild herbal tea (without caffeine) before bed can calm the mind.
- If severe, talk with a healthcare professional about how hormone therapies or certain supplements might help.

10.12 Building a Relaxing Bedtime Routine

A bedtime routine can help the brain and body transition from the busy day to a restful state. This might include:

1. **Warm Shower or Bath**: Rising body temperature and then cooling down can signal the body to get sleepy.
2. **Stretching or Yoga**: Gentle stretches can release tension in the muscles, including around the abdomen.
3. **Breathing Exercises**: Slow, deep breathing can calm the nervous system, which helps the gut feel less tense.
4. **Low-Level Lighting**: Switching off bright overhead lights and using a lamp can mimic sunset, telling the body it is nearing bedtime.

Such routines are not just for children. Adults can also benefit from signals that it is time for rest. Women who have difficulty sleeping can try different methods to see what fits best with their lifestyle.

10.13 Daily Breaks and Gut Calm

Rest is not only about sleep. Short breaks during the day can also help the gut. If you are always in a rush, the body stays in a "fight or flight" mode, which can slow digestion or make it less efficient. Stepping away from the computer or household tasks for a few minutes to breathe, stretch, or have a glass of water can reset stress levels.

Women who do not take breaks might find themselves overeating or craving sweets later as a response to stress or tiredness. Over time, that can lead to weight gain, energy crashes, and changes in gut bacteria. By taking small breaks, you give both the mind and gut a bit of space to regroup.

10.14 Routine for Meal Preparation

Meal prep can also reduce stress on the gut. If you have a routine for cooking or preparing meals, you are less likely to grab fast food or skip meals. This can help you avoid sudden hunger that leads to overeating. It can also ensure that fiber and nutrient intake remain consistent.

Possible meal prep ideas:

- Cook a batch of whole grains (like brown rice or quinoa) at the start of the week.
- Pre-chop vegetables so they are ready to toss into salads or stir-fries.
- Soak beans or lentils overnight to cook them faster the next day.
- Make extra portions of dinner to have as lunch the next day.

10.15 Screen Time and Gut Stress

Whether it is scrolling on social media or responding to endless work emails, screen time can keep the brain in a state of alertness. The emotional ups and downs that come with social media can also affect stress hormones, which in turn can affect digestion.

Setting a cutoff time each evening for non-essential screen use might improve sleep quality. Some women designate the hour before bed as a no-screen zone, opting for reading, knitting, or talking with family instead. This can calm the mind and help the body transition into rest mode.

10.16 Real-World Routines

- **Anna's Nighttime Checklist**: Anna found that writing a short checklist for the next day eased her mind. Once her worries about tasks were on paper, she slept better. She also noticed less morning stomach pain.
- **Riya's Lunchtime Walk**: Riya started using her lunch break to walk for 10 minutes outdoors. It gave her a mental break and stimulated her digestion. Over time, she felt more awake in the afternoon and had fewer cravings.
- **Sophia's Weekend Prep**: Sophia used Sundays to cook a large pot of vegetable soup and roast a tray of vegetables. She froze portions so she could quickly heat healthy meals during busy weekdays. She said this routine saved her from drive-through fast food.

10.17 Tips for Sustaining Restful Habits

1. **Start Small**: Instead of changing everything at once, pick one habit to work on, like going to bed 15 minutes earlier.
2. **Track Progress**: Using a journal or app to note when you went to bed or how you felt in the morning can show patterns over time.
3. **Reward Yourself**: If you manage a consistent sleep schedule for a week, you might plan a relaxing at-home foot soak or read a favorite (calming) book.
4. **Adjust as Needed**: Life changes, so your routine might need small updates. The key is to keep the core idea of consistent rest and meal timing.

10.18 Common Myths About Rest

1. **Myth**: Rest is lazy.
   Truth: Rest is necessary for cell repair, hormone balance, and mental clarity. Overwork without rest can lead to burnout and digestive upsets.

2. **Myth**: You can catch up on all lost sleep over the weekend.
   Truth: While sleeping in can help a bit, chronic sleep debt cannot be undone in a single day. Regular, adequate sleep is better in the long run.
3. **Myth**: If you lie in bed for a few hours, that counts as rest even if you did not sleep.
   Truth: Quiet time helps, but deep sleep has unique benefits. Aim for enough actual sleep each night.

10.19 Putting it All Together

A calm, well-rested body can handle daily stress better and keep digestion on track. Regular sleep promotes a healthy balance of hormones, which can reduce sudden cravings or mood swings that might affect meal choices. Paired with consistent meal times and short breaks during the day, rest can help keep the gut in a stable state.

Women often have full schedules and many responsibilities, but small steps toward a restful routine can go a long way. Even if you cannot change your workload, tweaking bedtimes, limiting screens, or adding a daily walk can help your gut feel more settled.

10.20 Conclusion to Chapter 10

Rest and routine are not luxuries; they are building blocks for a healthy gut. By honoring the body's need for sleep and daily structure, women can lessen digestive discomfort, maintain stable energy levels, and feel calmer overall. Setting realistic goals for bedtime, meal times, and regular breaks can turn rest into a powerful tool for supporting both mind and body.

In the next chapters, we will discuss food sensitivities, changes over the years, and other subjects that can affect gut health. Together, these insights can help women continue building a lifestyle that supports a comfortable and well-functioning digestive system.

Chapter 11

Food Sensitivities

Food sensitivities can confuse and frustrate many women. They may cause bloating, discomfort, skin issues, or other problems that seem to come out of nowhere. These sensitivities differ from full-blown allergies because they often do not trigger severe immune reactions like anaphylaxis. Instead, they can create ongoing discomfort or mild flare-ups. In this chapter, we will explore various types of food sensitivities, why women might be more prone to them, and how to test for and manage these issues.

11.1 What Are Food Sensitivities?

A food sensitivity occurs when the body has trouble breaking down or handling certain components in foods. Unlike a classic allergy (which is usually quick and involves a strong immune response), sensitivities can show up hours or even days after eating a problematic item. The symptoms can vary widely from person to person.

Common signals of a food sensitivity can include:

- Stomach pain or cramps
- Bloating and gas
- Diarrhea or constipation
- Skin rashes or acne
- Brain fog or reduced concentration
- Joint aches or mild swelling
- Headaches

While these might also appear in other conditions, if you notice a pattern tied to certain foods, it is worth looking deeper into the possibility of a sensitivity.

11.2 Types of Common Food Sensitivities

1. **Lactose Intolerance**
   Lactose is the sugar in milk. People with lactose intolerance lack enough of the enzyme lactase, which helps break down lactose in the small intestine. When lactose reaches the large intestine undigested, bacteria ferment it, leading to gas, bloating, and possibly diarrhea. Women who notice these signs after drinking milk or eating cheese might suspect lactose intolerance.
2. **Gluten Sensitivity**
   Gluten is a protein found in wheat, barley, and rye. Some individuals have celiac disease, which is an autoimmune disorder triggered by gluten. Others may have non-celiac gluten sensitivity, where eating gluten leads to stomach upset, headaches, or fatigue, but tests for celiac come back negative.
3. **FODMAP Intolerance**
   FODMAP stands for Fermentable Oligosaccharides, Disaccharides, Monosaccharides, and Polyols. These are carbohydrates that can be poorly absorbed in the small intestine. Foods high in FODMAPs include onions, garlic, wheat products, certain fruits (like apples), and some sweeteners (such as sorbitol). A high-FODMAP diet can lead to bloating and gas, especially for people with IBS.
4. **Histamine Intolerance**
   Histamine is a natural compound found in the body and in certain foods (like aged cheese, fermented products, and some fish). Usually, enzymes help break down extra histamine. But if these enzymes are not working well, high histamine levels might lead to headaches, flushing of the skin, or digestive symptoms.
5. **Other Sensitivities**
   Some women react badly to food additives, like certain colorings or preservatives. Others might have trouble with sulfites (found in dried fruits and wine). Each case can look different.

11.3 Why Women May Be More Susceptible

Hormonal shifts can change how the body processes food. Around the menstrual cycle, for instance, women might notice higher sensitivity to certain items. Stress can also be higher for women juggling multiple tasks, and stress can worsen gut issues. Hormones like progesterone may slow digestion, which can let certain sugars or proteins linger in the gut, giving bacteria more time to ferment them.

Women also tend to see doctors more often and may be more likely to notice subtle signs. This means they might pick up on a food sensitivity sooner than men. However, they can also be more prone to overthinking, which can lead to frustration when trying to identify what is causing discomfort.

11.4 Testing for Food Sensitivities

1. **Elimination Diet**
   One of the most straightforward methods is to remove suspected foods from your diet for two to four weeks and monitor changes. Then, you add them back one at a time to see if symptoms return. This requires patience and good record-keeping.
2. **Hydrogen Breath Tests**
   For lactose intolerance or some types of FODMAP issues, doctors might use a breath test. After consuming a specific sugar (like lactose or fructose), you breathe into a device that measures hydrogen. High hydrogen levels can suggest malabsorption and fermentation by gut bacteria.
3. **IgG Food Sensitivity Tests**
   Some labs offer tests that check IgG antibodies against certain foods. The science around these tests is debated. While some people find them helpful, others think they can give false positives. It is always best to speak with a knowledgeable professional before making major dietary changes based solely on these results.
4. **Celiac Disease Screening**
   If gluten is a concern, a doctor might first order blood tests for celiac disease (checking for certain antibodies). If these are positive, the next step might be an endoscopy to look at the small intestine. Women who suspect celiac should be tested before removing gluten from the diet, because going gluten-free beforehand can affect test results.

11.5 The Role of the Gut Barrier

The gut barrier is like a selective gatekeeper, letting nutrients pass into the bloodstream while keeping out harmful particles. If this barrier weakens, partly digested food can slip through, which might trigger immune responses or sensitivities.

Inflammation, poor diet, stress, and certain medications (like antibiotics or pain relievers) can reduce the integrity of this barrier. Women with hormone imbalances or chronic stress might see a higher risk of a leaky gut. A leaky gut is not an official medical diagnosis, but the concept helps explain how sensitivities or immune-related concerns can start.

11.6 Managing Food Sensitivities

1. **Identify Triggers**
   Keep a simple food diary, noting what you eat and any symptoms that follow. Patterns may emerge, such as stomach pain after ice cream or headaches after wine.
2. **Remove or Reduce**
   If you find a clear pattern, consider removing that food or reducing it. Sometimes, a small amount might be okay, but a large amount triggers problems. For instance, someone with mild lactose intolerance might tolerate yogurt or hard cheese but not a glass of milk.
3. **Try Alternatives**
    - Lactose-free milk or dairy substitutes (almond milk, soy milk, etc.)
    - Gluten-free grains like rice, quinoa, or buckwheat
    - FODMAP-friendly vegetables (such as bok choy or bell peppers) if you suspect high-FODMAP items are a problem
    - Low-histamine options if histamine is the issue
4. **Support Gut Health**
   A varied diet with enough fiber, along with probiotics or fermented foods (if tolerated), can help strengthen the gut barrier. For some women, focusing on general gut support can reduce the intensity of sensitivities over time.

11.7 Balancing Nutrients on a Restricted Diet

One concern with removing certain foods is the risk of missing out on key nutrients. For example, if you cut out dairy, you may lose a major source of calcium. If you eliminate wheat, you might miss out on certain B vitamins and fiber.

Steps to maintain balance:

- Check labels for fortification (e.g., calcium-fortified plant milk).
- Include a variety of fruits, vegetables, legumes, and grains to fill nutritional gaps.
- Consider working with a dietitian if your restrictions are extensive.
- Use supplements when needed, but make sure you choose them carefully and speak to a professional if unsure.

11.8 The Link Between Sensitivities and Stress

Food sensitivities and stress can fuel each other. If you are stressed, digestion might slow, leading to more fermentation of carbs or incomplete breakdown of proteins. This can raise the chance of discomfort. Stress also affects the gut barrier, making it more porous.

On the flip side, dealing with ongoing stomach trouble can create more stress or anxiety. Over time, a cycle can form where each problem feeds into the other. Addressing stress is just as crucial as managing the sensitivity itself. This might involve relaxation methods, counseling, or lifestyle changes that reduce daily tension.

11.9 Social and Emotional Challenges

Dealing with sensitivities can be tricky in social settings. You might worry about going to a restaurant or a friend's house if you are not sure what is in the food. Some people feel embarrassed asking about ingredients or making special requests.

Tips for managing socially:

- Inform hosts or friends ahead of time about significant restrictions.
- Offer to bring a dish you can safely eat.
- Learn how to read menus carefully. Ask about sauces or marinades that might contain hidden triggers.
- Practice short ways to explain your sensitivity without feeling awkward. For example, "I need to avoid dairy because my stomach does not handle it well."

Emotional support can be helpful. Connecting with others who face similar challenges (through support groups or forums) can remind you that you are not alone. If anxiety about food becomes intense, seeking professional help could improve mental health and life quality.

11.10 Food Sensitivities During Pregnancy or Hormonal Shifts

Pregnancy can change how the body responds to certain foods. Some women who had lactose intolerance before pregnancy find they can handle dairy better for a while, while others discover new sensitivities. Hormonal shifts can also make tastes or smells more intense.

Similarly, during perimenopause or menopause, changing hormone levels can alter digestion speed and gut bacteria. Foods that used to be fine may start causing trouble. Keeping track of these changes and staying flexible can help. If you sense new patterns, consider an elimination approach or talk to a healthcare provider for guidance.

11.11 The Difference Between Sensitivity and Allergy

A true food allergy involves the immune system making IgE antibodies against a specific food protein. Symptoms usually appear quickly and can include hives, swelling, breathing issues, or anaphylaxis. This is a medical emergency.

Food sensitivities, on the other hand, typically involve more subtle responses that can build up over time. They might relate to IgG or other immune pathways, or they might simply be the result of enzyme problems (as with lactose). Understanding this difference is crucial. If you suspect a food allergy, a professional evaluation and the potential need for emergency medication (like an EpiPen) is vital.

11.12 Rotation Diet and Other Approaches

Some people use a rotation diet, where they only eat certain food groups on specific days, then rotate. This can reduce constant exposure to the same items. If the gut is reacting due to overexposure, a rotation diet might help break the cycle. However, it can be complicated to maintain.

Other approaches can include:

- **Low-FODMAP Diet**: Often used for IBS or strong bloating. This diet involves removing high-FODMAP foods, then reintroducing them in phases.
- **Low-Histamine Diet**: Removing aged cheeses, fermented foods, cured meats, and so on to see if headaches or skin flares improve.
- **GAPS or Specific Carbohydrate Diet**: Some people try these to manage tricky gut issues, but they can be quite restrictive.

Always approach strict diets cautiously. If you cut out many food groups, watch for nutrient deficits. Some diets may help for a period, but are not meant to be lifelong unless strictly necessary (as in celiac disease).

11.13 Monitoring and Adjusting Over Time

What triggers symptoms in one phase of life might change later. A woman could have had no issues with dairy until her early 30s, then suddenly struggle. Or she might only find certain foods bother her when she is under high stress. Periodic check-ins can help keep track of these shifts.

If you suspect a sensitivity is easing (for example, you took a break from gluten, and now small amounts no longer cause pain), you can gently test tolerance levels. Sometimes the gut heals enough with better overall care and stress management, letting you enjoy foods in moderation again.

11.14 Self-Care Beyond Food

Managing food sensitivities is about more than just what is on your plate. It involves a range of self-care practices to keep the gut calm and the mind at ease:

- **Adequate Sleep**: Deep rest allows the gut to repair.
- **Physical Activity**: Movement helps speed up digestion and reduce stress hormones.
- **Hydration**: Water assists in breaking down foods and helps maintain gut lining integrity.
- **Stress Management**: Chronic stress can intensify gut issues. Techniques such as breathing exercises, gentle stretching, and short breaks can help.

11.15 Myths Around Food Sensitivities

1. **Myth**: They are all in the head.
   Fact: While stress and mindset can affect digestion, many sensitivities have real physical roots. Women should trust their bodies if they notice consistent patterns.
2. **Myth**: An IgG test is enough to diagnose everything.
   Fact: IgG tests are debated among experts. Some see them as a clue, but not a definite result. Elimination diets and professional advice often provide clearer insights.
3. **Myth**: A single food sensitivity is permanent.
   Fact: Some go away after gut healing, while others (such as celiac disease) are for life. It depends on the nature of the sensitivity.

11.16 Steps to Take if You Suspect a Sensitivity

1. **Observe**: Keep a small notebook or use a simple phone app to list meals, snacks, and symptoms.
2. **Seek Guidance**: A doctor or dietitian can help confirm concerns or rule out other causes.
3. **Eliminate Safely**: If you remove an entire food group, find substitutes or supplements to avoid nutrient losses.
4. **Test and Reintroduce**: After a period of avoidance, carefully reintroduce small amounts. Notice if symptoms return.
5. **Keep Evolving**: Monitor changes over time. Sensitivities are not always static.

11.17 Helping Children or Teens with Sensitivities

Some women are parents who might notice similar issues in their kids. While the focus of this book is on women's gut health, it is worth noting that children can also develop intolerances. Girls, especially, might experience changes during puberty when hormones shift.

If you suspect a child has a sensitivity, speak with a pediatrician or a specialist before making big dietary changes. Children need a broad range of nutrients to grow, so a well-structured approach is key.

11.18 Travel and Food Sensitivities

Travel can make sticking to a restricted diet tricky. Here are some ways to cope:

- **Plan Ahead**: Research restaurants, grocery stores, or local markets at your destination.
- **Carry Safe Snacks**: Bring items like gluten-free crackers, lactose-free milk powder, or dried fruit (if tolerated) to avoid last-minute junk food.
- **Learn Key Phrases**: If traveling abroad, know how to explain your sensitivity in the local language.

- **Be Flexible**: You might not find perfect options, so focus on doing the best you can. If a slip happens, have a plan for dealing with symptoms (like certain teas or over-the-counter aids).

11.19 Emotional Wellbeing and Mindful Eating

When you have a food sensitivity, it can be easy to develop fear or anxiety around eating. This might lead to social withdrawal or over-restriction. Mindful eating can help you pay attention to your body's signals without becoming overly fearful:

- **Eat Slowly**: Chew each bite fully and notice flavors.
- **Avoid Distractions**: Put away phones or screens during meals so you can tune in to how your stomach feels.
- **Pause and Observe**: Partway through a meal, pause to see if you feel satisfied or still hungry.

Being aware does not mean panicking over every bite. It is about giving your gut time to communicate with you.

11.20 Conclusion to Chapter 11

Food sensitivities are a complex area, especially for women whose bodies go through regular changes. Recognizing common signs, testing carefully, and making thoughtful dietary adjustments can help reduce discomfort. Still, it is not just about the foods themselves—stress, gut barrier health, and hormones also play major roles.

With patience, record-keeping, and sometimes guidance from a specialist, many women learn to manage or reduce sensitivities. In some cases, removing or limiting certain foods can bring significant relief, letting the gut function better. In others, careful reintroduction may be possible down the line.

Chapter 12

Changes Over the Years

A woman's body goes through many phases, each bringing shifts in hormones, metabolism, and gut function. From the teenage years to later life, these changes can affect how the body processes nutrients, how quickly digestion happens, and how strong the gut barrier remains. In this chapter, we will look at how the gut can alter over time and what women can do to handle each stage with more ease.

12.1 Early Years and Teen Stage

During childhood and the teenage years, the digestive system develops and adapts to different foods. Teen years bring a wave of hormones like estrogen and progesterone, which can affect hunger and digestion. Some teenagers notice more frequent stomach pains or changes in bowel habits around the start of menstruation.

Nutritional demands are high in adolescence because of growth spurts and bone development. Teens need enough protein, calcium, iron, and other nutrients. At the same time, peer pressure and busy school schedules can push them to eat more fast food or skip meals. When combined with hormonal shifts, poor eating habits can increase the risk of constipation, gas, or even early signs of IBS.

Advice for Teenagers and Parents:

- Encourage balanced meals with fruits, vegetables, and whole grains.
- Limit sugary drinks and ultra-processed snacks.
- Ensure enough calcium and vitamin D for bone growth.
- Talk about how stress from exams or social issues can affect digestion.

12.2 Early Adulthood: Twenties and Early Thirties

As women move into their twenties and early thirties, the body tends to be at its peak in terms of metabolism and healing capacity. However, this is also a time when many face hectic schedules, job stress, or the start of family responsibilities.

Some women may notice new digestive issues if they change their eating patterns drastically—such as switching to fad diets or relying on convenience foods. Others might start birth control, which can alter hormone levels and possibly affect digestion.

Key Points:

- Listen to body signals: If certain foods begin to cause discomfort, do not ignore it.
- Stay hydrated: Long work hours can lead to forgetting to drink water.
- Build regular meal times: Skipping meals or late-night snacking may disrupt the circadian rhythm.

12.3 Pregnancy and Postpartum

Pregnancy brings major hormonal changes. The growing baby demands nutrients, and progesterone levels rise significantly. This hormone can slow the muscles that move food through the intestines, leading to constipation. As the uterus expands, it may press on the stomach and intestines, making heartburn or acid reflux more common.

Some pregnant women also develop cravings or aversions. They might crave sweets or feel turned off by meats or vegetables they once loved. Morning sickness (which can occur any time of day) can affect appetite and nutrient intake.

After birth, hormone levels drop rapidly, which can trigger changes in mood and digestion. If the mother is breastfeeding, the body uses extra energy to produce milk, requiring more fluids and nutrients. Some women experience bowel irregularities for weeks after delivery.

Tips During Pregnancy and Postpartum:

- Include fiber-rich foods, like oats or fruits, to help prevent constipation.
- Focus on small, frequent meals if heartburn is a problem.
- Stay active in gentle ways (like walking), which can aid digestion.
- Drink enough water, especially when breastfeeding.
- Seek help if mood changes or digestive troubles become overwhelming.

12.4 Midlife: Thirties to Forties

In the midlife stage, women often juggle careers, families, and household responsibilities. Chronic stress can become a major factor, and this stress can harm gut health by raising cortisol levels and disturbing normal digestion.

Many women also notice fluctuations in menstrual cycles as they inch closer to perimenopause. These shifts in hormones can cause more pronounced changes in bowel habits, bloating, or sensitivity to certain foods. Some might see an increase in weight around the belly, which can add pressure on the digestive organs.

Self-Care at This Stage:

- Stress management is important. Short breaks, basic breathing techniques, or brisk walks can reduce tension.
- Meal planning can help avoid quick junk food choices. Cooking in batches on weekends can make healthy meals easier on busy weekdays.
- Be aware of new sensitivities or changes in digestion as hormone levels begin to fluctuate.

12.5 Perimenopause and Menopause

Perimenopause is the transition leading up to menopause, when estrogen and progesterone production starts to vary more widely. This stage can last for several years. Menopause is confirmed after 12 months without a menstrual period.

How does this affect the gut?

- Estrogen helps maintain the health of many tissues, including the gut lining. As estrogen drops, some women may see shifts in gut bacteria and changes in bowel habits.
- Hot flashes, night sweats, or trouble sleeping can lead to more stress or fatigue, which impacts digestion.
- Weight might redistribute, often settling around the waist, which can add to heartburn or reflux.

Ways to Manage Perimenopause and Menopause:

- Include a balance of protein, healthy fats, and fiber to help maintain stable blood sugar and support gut bacteria.
- Aim for calcium and vitamin D to support bone health, since bone loss speeds up when estrogen levels fall.
- Consider discussing hormone therapy or other measures with a healthcare provider if symptoms are severe. Some women find that adjusting hormone levels also helps with digestive comfort.

12.6 Postmenopause and Later Life

After menopause, estrogen levels remain low, which can continue to shape gut function. Muscle mass tends to decline with age, including the muscles in the intestines. This can slow bowel movements, raising the chance of constipation.

In older age, certain medicines (like blood pressure drugs or painkillers) can also disrupt normal digestion. Reduced activity levels can mean less blood flow to the gut and slower motility.

Strategies for Healthy Digestion in Later Life:

- Keep up with gentle exercise, such as walking or stretching, to support circulation and muscle tone.
- Eat enough protein to maintain muscle mass, including the muscles in the digestive tract.
- Address dryness issues. Some older women notice dryness in many tissues, including the mouth, which can affect chewing. Sipping water between bites may help.
- Watch for vitamin B12 levels, as absorption can drop with age.

12.7 Changes in Gut Microbes with Age

Research shows that the variety of gut bacteria can shift as we grow older. Some groups of bacteria may increase, while others decrease, depending on diet, medications, and overall health. Lower diversity in gut microbes is linked to a higher risk of digestive problems or infections.

Supporting Bacterial Diversity:

- Eat a range of vegetables, fruits, whole grains, legumes, nuts, and seeds.
- Include fermented foods (like yogurt, kefir, or sauerkraut) if tolerated, to add beneficial microbes.
- Limit overuse of antibiotics, as they can reduce healthy bacterial populations.
- Stay active, as exercise can support a more varied microbiome.

12.8 Hormones Throughout the Years

1. **Estrogen**
    - In teen years, estrogen rises to help develop female traits and regulate menstrual cycles.
    - During reproductive years, estrogen fluctuates monthly. It helps maintain bone density and skin elasticity.

- As perimenopause begins, estrogen levels can swing, leading to symptoms like hot flashes.
- After menopause, estrogen stays low, which may affect the gut lining and metabolism.

2. **Progesterone**
   - Also rises in puberty, peaks during the second half of each cycle, and plays a role in pregnancy.
   - Can slow digestion, leading to constipation if levels are high.
   - Drops after menopause, removing its calming effects on the nervous system and possibly changing bowel habits.

3. **Cortisol**
   - Stress hormone that can stay elevated if life pressure is constant, affecting digestion at any stage of life.

Understanding these hormonal swings can help women see how their gut changes might be normal responses to different life phases.

12.9 Adjusting Nutrient Needs Over Time

Women's nutrient needs do not stay the same. For example, younger women need enough iron to replace what is lost during menstruation. After menopause, iron requirements may decrease if there is no monthly loss of blood.

- **Calcium and Vitamin D**: Important throughout life but especially after age 50 to reduce bone density loss.
- **Protein**: May need to be higher in older adulthood to maintain muscle mass.
- **Fiber**: Remains vital at all stages to keep digestion regular and support good bacteria.
- **Omega-3 Fats**: May help reduce inflammation, which can rise with age.

12.10 Lifestyle Changes for Different Decades

1. **20s-30s**:
    - Set a base of healthy eating and regular exercise.
    - Identify any mild sensitivities early.
    - Make sure you get enough iron and folate if you plan to have children.
2. **40s**:
    - Watch stress levels, as they can peak with work and family.
    - Adjust portion sizes if metabolism slows.
    - Remain aware of hormonal changes that might affect gut comfort.
3. **50s and Beyond**:
    - Stay active with low-impact exercise like walking, swimming, or gentle yoga.
    - Check bone density. Consider calcium, vitamin D, and possibly magnesium to keep bones and muscles in good shape.
    - Review any long-term medications with a doctor to see if they affect digestion.

12.11 Shifts in Appetite and Cravings

At different life phases, appetite can go up or down due to hormones, stress, or changes in daily activity. For example, pregnancy can cause unusual cravings, while menopause might bring sugar cravings if mood is low or sleep is poor.

Listening to these cravings without letting them run your life can be a balancing act. If you crave sweets, sometimes a piece of fruit or a small square of dark chocolate can be enough to satisfy you. If the craving persists, it might be a clue about emotional needs or a nutritional gap.

12.12 Mental Wellbeing Across the Years

As women age, responsibilities and stressors can change. Raising children (if that applies), caring for aging parents, or adjusting to an "empty nest" can all affect mental state. Depression or anxiety can arise at any age, and these feelings can worsen digestive issues.

Hormonal dips or spikes can influence mood. For instance, some women experience anxiety around perimenopause. Having strategies to cope—such as counseling, mild exercise, or social support—can ease gut symptoms linked to emotional ups and downs.

12.13 The Role of Body Composition Changes

Throughout life, muscle mass tends to peak in the twenties and starts a slow decline after the thirties if not maintained. Less muscle mass can lower metabolism, making weight gain more likely if eating habits do not adjust. Extra weight around the abdomen can squeeze digestive organs and raise the risk of acid reflux or a sluggish bowel.

Including resistance exercises (like light weightlifting or resistance bands) can preserve muscle, helping to keep the gut active and supported. Protein intake is also crucial. Even older women can build and maintain muscle with the right diet and consistent activity.

12.14 Menopause Hormone Therapy and Digestion

Some women consider hormone therapy during perimenopause or after menopause to reduce hot flashes or other symptoms. This involves taking estrogen or a mix of estrogen and progesterone.

For some, hormone therapy might help with vaginal dryness or bone health, but it also comes with risks. Digestion-wise, adjusting estrogen can affect how the gut moves or how bacteria behave. Women on hormone therapy might notice subtle changes in bowel habits. It is important to have ongoing check-ups to make sure the therapy does not lead to unwanted side effects.

12.15 Practical Ways to Adapt

- **Stay Curious**: At each new stage, watch for changes in digestion. If you see a pattern of discomfort, bloating, or new sensitivities, try slight diet adjustments or speak with a professional.
- **Focus on Fiber and Fluids**: These two remain key at every age. They keep bowel movements regular, feed good bacteria, and help flush out waste.
- **Exercise Wisely**: Choose activities that match your fitness level and stage of life. Even a 20-minute walk each day can support digestion and mood.
- **Adjust Serving Sizes**: Metabolism usually slows with age, so portion control can help avoid weight gain and the gut problems that can come with it.
- **Check Nutrient Levels**: Blood tests can confirm if you are low in vitamin D, iron, B12, or other key nutrients. This is especially important if you have changed your diet.

12.16 The Impact of Medical Conditions

Chronic conditions often appear more as we get older. Diabetes, high blood pressure, or thyroid disorders can all affect gut health. Women with autoimmune conditions might find their symptoms change during pregnancy or menopause.

If you take regular medications, check for possible side effects on digestion. For example, some pain relievers can cause constipation, while certain diabetes drugs can speed up bowel movements. Balancing medication needs with gut comfort might require some trial and error under a doctor's guidance.

12.17 Mental Approach to Aging

How you view the aging process can influence your choices. Some women see age as a reason to slow down or expect ill health. Others adapt by staying active, learning new activities, or focusing on a nutrient-rich diet. A positive outlook can reduce stress hormones, which in turn helps the gut.

Taking care of mental wellbeing—through hobbies, social ties, or mindfulness—can keep the gut less stressed. This can improve bowel regularity and might help manage weight or cravings.

12.18 Home Environment and Assistance

In older years, it might become harder to cook daily meals or shop for fresh produce. Finding ways to get help is key. Some women move to smaller homes, senior communities, or live with family. Others use grocery delivery or meal services.

Even younger women might face times when a busy schedule prevents cooking. Preparing and freezing meals or using a meal kit service for healthy ingredients can bridge that gap. Adaptation at each stage can help you keep your digestion running well without sacrificing convenience.

12.19 Celebrating Each Stage

Each stage of life has benefits and difficulties. The teenage years bring growth, while the twenties and thirties can be full of new experiences. The forties and fifties might include balancing work and family. Later decades can provide more free time for hobbies if retirement is an option.

In each stage, the gut remains a central part of overall health. By noticing how digestion changes and adapting your eating, movement, and stress management, you can find more comfort. There is no single method that works for every woman, but listening to your body is always wise.

12.20 Conclusion to Chapter 12

Women's bodies do not stay the same over time. Hormones shift, metabolism changes, and stress levels go up or down. All these factors can shape how the gut works. From the challenges of puberty to the changes of menopause and beyond, each life phase requires attention to diet, activity, and self-care.

By recognizing how these shifts can affect digestion, women can stay ahead of common problems like bloating, constipation, or new food sensitivities. Small steps—such as adding more fiber, tweaking meal times, including daily movement, and managing stress—can go a long way in protecting gut health at every stage.

In the chapters ahead, we will explore more connections between mood and the gut, how exercise ties into digestive comfort, the effects of toxins, and how to address women's health issues tied to digestion. By staying informed and open to adjusting habits, it is possible to keep the gut feeling well-supported, no matter the age or phase of life you are in.

Chapter 13

How the Gut Affects Mood

Women often talk about feeling uneasy in the stomach when worried, or getting excited "butterflies" before an important event. These are common phrases, but they hint at a deeper reality: the gut is closely connected to mood and emotional wellbeing. For many years, people thought that the brain controlled everything. Today, studies show that the gut also sends signals to the brain, influencing how we think and feel. This chapter looks at how the gut can affect mood, what can go wrong, and how to keep this connection steady for better emotional balance.

13.1 The Gut-Brain Loop

The human body has multiple communication networks, but the link between the gut and the brain stands out. This two-way loop uses nerves, hormones, and chemical messengers. While chapter 6 looked at the "brain-gut connection," here we focus on the ways the gut itself can drive changes in mood, rather than just how the brain might affect the gut.

1. **Nerve Pathways**:
   One major route is the vagus nerve, which sends signals from the digestive tract to the brain. These signals can be about how full we are, the state of microbial balance, or if there is inflammation. The brain then interprets these signals, which can shift mood or energy levels.
2. **Chemical Messengers**:
   The gut produces many chemicals, including serotonin and dopamine. Though these chemicals are often linked to the brain, a large amount of serotonin is actually made in the gut. When the gut lining or microbe balance is off, serotonin production can shift, influencing how we feel.
3. **Immune System Signals**:
   Much of the body's immune system lies in the gut. If the gut lining is weak or inflamed, immune signals can reach the brain, possibly contributing to low mood or anxious feelings.

When everything works correctly, these signals help the brain track digestion and keep mood stable. But if gut health is poor, the signals can become unbalanced, leading to emotional strain.

13.2 Why the Gut Can Shift Mood in Women

Women may notice mood changes more strongly than men when the gut is unhappy. Several factors can play a role:

1. **Hormone Swings**:
   Women's hormone levels, such as estrogen and progesterone, change throughout the monthly cycle and across life stages. These hormones can affect how nerve cells respond to signals from the gut. For instance, times of low estrogen might link to a dip in certain feel-good chemicals.
2. **Stress and Responsibilities**:
   Women often handle multiple tasks, from jobs to caregiving. Chronic stress can weaken the gut barrier, allowing more inflammation. This can lead to a cycle where stress harms the gut, and an unhealthy gut increases stress signals.
3. **Nutrient Demands**:
   In certain phases, like pregnancy or breastfeeding, the body prioritizes nutrients for the baby. If the mother's diet is lacking, her gut might suffer. That can lead to mood changes because of reduced serotonin or other chemical messengers.
4. **Social Factors**:
   Women sometimes feel more pressure to meet expectations, which can lead to hidden stress. This tension influences hormones like cortisol, which then affects the gut's environment and can lead to emotional ups and downs.

13.3 Serotonin and the "Feel-Good" Connection

Serotonin is a key chemical for mood regulation. Low levels are linked to sadness or worry, while balanced levels help with calmness and a steady mood. Surprisingly, the gut produces the majority of the body's serotonin. This does not mean all gut-made serotonin goes straight to the brain, but it plays a big role in signaling and overall balance.

- **Production**: Specialized cells in the gut lining make serotonin in response to food intake, microbial signals, and other factors.
- **Impact on Gut Movement**: Serotonin also helps manage how quickly food passes through the digestive tract. Shifts in serotonin can cause diarrhea or constipation, which can then influence mood again.
- **Microbe Support**: Certain gut bacteria help the body make or absorb serotonin's building blocks. If these microbes are lacking, the body may not produce enough serotonin.

Women who sense they are more emotionally reactive at certain times might look at diet or gut health. Simple changes—like adding more fiber or fermented foods—could help the body maintain better serotonin balance.

13.4 Dopamine and Pleasure Signals

Dopamine is another chemical that affects motivation and pleasure. While the brain is the main site for dopamine's mood effects, some of it is produced or regulated by gut bacteria. If the gut microbiome is unbalanced, the signals for dopamine might not be sent or received correctly, possibly leading to low motivation or a sense of being "down."

For example, some studies on mice show that when certain gut bacteria are missing, dopamine levels in the brain can drop. Though humans are more complex, early findings suggest that a similar pattern could happen. Women who notice a slump in mood might consider how their gut is doing. Chronic diarrhea, constipation, or unexplained bloating may point to microbiome problems that also influence dopamine.

13.5 Gut Inflammation and Mood Problems

Inflammation in the gut can sometimes spread signals that lead to mood issues. When the gut lining is irritated, immune cells release substances called cytokines. These can travel through the bloodstream, possibly passing signals that the brain interprets as stress or threat.

1. **Leaky Gut Effects**:
   If the gut barrier becomes too porous, more unwanted elements can slip into the bloodstream. The immune system then responds strongly, creating more inflammation. Over time, this process can be tied to ongoing low mood or feelings of worry.
2. **Dietary Triggers**:
   Diets high in sugar, unhealthy fats, or processed items can lead to a gut environment that encourages inflammation. For women who already have hormone swings, adding inflammation can make mood dips more intense.
3. **Chronic Inflammatory Issues**:
   Conditions like irritable bowel syndrome (IBS) or inflammatory bowel disease (IBD) can amplify this effect. Women who have these conditions often report feeling more emotionally sensitive or struggling with low mood.

13.6 Food Choices That Influence Mood

Certain foods can help the gut produce beneficial chemicals or reduce inflammation, while others can do the opposite. Women often have the power to make simple but powerful changes in daily meals to support a more stable mood. Below are some guiding points:

1. **Probiotic-Rich Items**:
   Yogurt (with live cultures), kefir, and some fermented vegetables can add beneficial bacteria. These bacteria may help produce calming chemicals or reduce inflammation, contributing to better emotional steadiness.
2. **High-Fiber Foods**:
   Foods like beans, oats, berries, and flaxseeds feed good gut

microbes, helping with stable gut function. Steady gut function often means fewer mood swings linked to bloating or constipation.
3. **Omega-3 Fats**:
Found in fish like salmon or sardines, these fats can help reduce inflammation and support brain cell health. Including them a few times a week might support mood and gut stability.
4. **Limit Sugar and Ultra-Processed Foods**:
Too much sugar can cause a spike and then crash in energy, affecting mood. These foods can also feed less helpful bacteria in the gut, which might lead to more inflammation over time.
5. **Hydration**:
While water itself is not a direct mood booster, dehydration can worsen stress on the body. Drinking enough water helps the gut process nutrients and remove waste more easily.

13.7 How Stress Management Aids the Gut-Mood Link

Stress is not only about feeling tense. It triggers hormone releases that can make the gut more sensitive or inflamed. Over time, chronic stress can reduce the variety of gut microbes, opening the door to mood problems. Taking steps to manage stress can protect both the gut and the mind.

1. **Slow Breathing Exercises**:
Breathing in through the nose for a count of four and out through the mouth for a count of four helps calm the nervous system. This can reduce cortisol, a stress hormone that harms the gut over time.
2. **Gentle Movement**:
Activities like walking or mild stretching can lower stress hormones and improve circulation. Better circulation can help the gut receive nutrients and clear out waste, which supports more stable mood signals.
3. **Setting Boundaries**:
Women often carry emotional loads from work, family, or social events. Learning to say "no" to extra tasks when feeling overloaded can prevent chronic stress. A lower stress level usually means happier gut microbes.

4. **Taking Short Breaks**:
   Breaking up busy days with short relaxation periods (even if it is just a few minutes of quiet) helps the mind reset. This keeps stress from stacking up and harming the gut.

13.8 Sleep Quality and Gut-Driven Mood

Poor sleep can hurt gut health, and an unhappy gut can make it harder to sleep well, leading to a cycle. When the gut does not rest properly, it may produce fewer mood-supporting chemicals or let more inflammation flare up at night. Women who often sacrifice sleep due to caregiving or work might notice more mood swings.

- **Sleep Hormones**: Melatonin is known for regulating sleep, but it is also produced in the gut. A gut out of balance might affect melatonin levels, which can lead to restless nights.
- **Routine**: Going to bed at a stable time and avoiding heavy meals close to bedtime can give the gut a chance to do its repair work. This often translates to steadier mood the next day.

13.9 Managing Gut-Related Mood Slumps

When mood slumps happen alongside gut symptoms, it might help to have a plan:

1. **Track Patterns**:
   Keep a simple journal listing how you feel each day, what you ate, and any digestion issues. Over time, see if certain meals or stress events line up with mood dips.
2. **Try a Gut-Friendly Reset**:
   If bloating or discomfort seems tied to low mood, consider focusing on gut-friendly foods (like soups with vegetables and mild spices, or yogurt with berries) for a few days. Avoid known triggers like spicy sauces or sugary drinks.

3. **Use Mild Herbal Support**:
   Some herbal teas, like chamomile or peppermint (unless reflux is present), can soothe the stomach. Reducing stomach tension may indirectly help calm nerves.
4. **Seek Help if Needed**:
   If mood problems persist, it might be helpful to speak with a therapist or counselor. They can help manage stressors that circle back to the gut. Likewise, a gastroenterologist or dietitian can look for deeper causes of digestive trouble.

13.10 Golden Tips for a Better Gut-Mood Balance

1. **Listen to Early Warnings**:
   If you suddenly have unusual bowel changes and find yourself more anxious or down, it could be a clue that something in the gut needs attention. Early action can keep problems from growing.
2. **Focus on Variety**:
   Eating a wide range of whole foods (fruits, vegetables, grains, proteins) keeps the gut microbiome diverse. A diverse microbiome sends more balanced signals to the brain, supporting better mood.
3. **Balanced Blood Sugar**:
   A big blood sugar spike, followed by a crash, can make women feel jittery or low. Pairing carbohydrates with protein and healthy fat at meals helps prevent extreme highs or lows.
4. **Limit Overuse of Antibiotics**:
   Antibiotics can wipe out the helpful bacteria that support mood-regulating chemicals. Use antibiotics only when truly necessary, and consider taking a probiotic afterward to restore microbial balance.
5. **Watch Caffeine**:
   A moderate amount of caffeine might be fine, but too much can raise stress hormones and irritate the gut lining, leading to mood jitters or even extra bathroom visits.
6. **Stay Curious**:
   Each woman's body is different. What works for one might not work for another. Staying open-minded and ready to adapt can help find the best path for personal gut and mood health.

Putting It All Together

The gut can shape a woman's emotional life in real ways. Serotonin, dopamine, and other chemicals made in or regulated by the gut send signals that reach the brain. When the gut is balanced, these signals can create a sense of calm or contentment. When the gut is inflamed, lacking key nutrients, or overrun by less helpful microbes, it can lead to mood changes such as sadness, worry, or irritability.

Several lifestyle choices—like eating a range of nutrient-rich foods, managing stress, and keeping a regular sleep schedule—can help maintain a healthy gut. Tracking patterns in food intake and mood can provide insights into whether certain items trigger negative reactions. Simple steps, such as adding more fiber or cutting back on sugary treats, might improve both gut comfort and emotional steadiness.

Women should keep in mind that mood shifts can have many causes. Hormones, social factors, and mental stress all work together with gut health. By viewing the gut as a partner in emotional wellbeing, it may be easier to spot patterns and take action before small problems become major ones.

Chapter 14

Physical Activity and Digestion

Many people look at exercise mainly as a way to manage weight or build muscle. While these are valid goals, physical activity also plays a key role in how the gut works. Simple movement can help the intestines move food along, reduce inflammation, and even improve the balance of gut microbes. For women, who often face shifts in hormones and stress levels, being active can ease common digestive troubles like bloating, gas, or constipation. This chapter explores why exercise is so helpful for digestion, how different types of activity might help, and practical ways to fit movement into a busy schedule.

14.1 Why Physical Activity Matters for the Gut

1. **Movement Aids Bowel Flow**:
   The muscles in the intestines contract to push food through. Regular physical activity can help these muscles stay toned and active. When women become more sedentary, the bowels often slow down, leading to constipation or incomplete emptying.
2. **Better Blood Circulation**:
   Exercise boosts heart rate and blood flow. More blood flowing to the digestive tract can enhance nutrient absorption and help remove waste. This can reduce the strain on the gut if it is having trouble getting enough oxygen or nutrients.
3. **Stress Relief**:
   Physical activity releases chemicals like endorphins, which can lower stress. Since high stress can upset gut balance, lowering it through exercise is a bonus.
4. **Microbial Changes**:
   Some studies show that exercise can raise the variety of gut microbes, which is usually a sign of good health. A more diverse microbiome can handle a broader range of foods without negative reactions.

14.2 Types of Physical Activity and Their Effects

Not all exercise is the same. Women can benefit in different ways, depending on the form of movement:

1. **Walking**:
   A brisk 20-30 minute walk can help digestion. Each step gently shakes the organs in the abdomen, helping food move along. Walking is easy on the joints, so it is a good choice for women who want a low-impact activity.
2. **Jogging or Running**:
   This more intense cardio can increase gut motility, but some women find that running too soon after a meal leads to discomfort. If running is part of a routine, spacing out meals by an hour or two can help prevent cramps or stomach aches.
3. **Yoga or Stretching**:
   Certain yoga poses, like twists or gentle bends, can stimulate the digestive organs. This can reduce gas or bloating. For women under stress, yoga also calms the mind, lowering cortisol that can harm the gut.
4. **Strength Training**:
   Building muscle through resistance exercises (such as lifting weights or using resistance bands) can help the core and support posture. Good posture means less pressure on the digestive organs, possibly lowering reflux or heartburn episodes.
5. **Pilates**:
   Pilates focuses on strengthening the core muscles, which include the abdomen and lower back. A stronger core can mean better support for the intestines, improved posture, and possibly fewer digestive complaints.

14.3 Best Practices for Timing Exercise and Meals

1. **Before Meals**:
   Some people prefer a quick walk or light activity before eating to improve appetite and clear the mind. However, intense workouts on

an empty stomach may cause nausea in those prone to low blood sugar.
2. **Right After Meals**:
Strenuous exercise immediately after a big meal can cause cramps or even reflux, as blood flow is still directed to the digestive system. A gentle stroll, though, can help with digestion without stressing the body.
3. **Between Meals**:
Many find it comfortable to work out an hour or two after eating. The stomach is not too full, and the body has some fuel available. This timing may reduce the chance of cramps or bowel discomfort during the workout.
4. **Late Evenings**:
Exercising close to bedtime might energize the body, making it harder to sleep. If you only have time at night, consider calmer activities like gentle yoga instead of high-intensity cardio.

14.4 How Exercise Can Ease Constipation

Constipation is a common complaint for women, especially during times of high progesterone or stress. Physical activity can help by:

1. **Increasing Muscle Contractions**:
Activities such as brisk walking or light aerobics encourage the large intestine to contract more often, helping waste move along.
2. **Preventing a Sedentary Cycle**:
Sitting for long hours can slow bowel movement. Breaking up sitting with short bursts of stretching or walking can stimulate the gut.
3. **Boosting Water Intake**:
People who exercise tend to drink more water. Better hydration makes stools softer and easier to pass.

If constipation is chronic, combining exercise with fiber-rich foods and enough fluids can bring relief. It may take time for the body to adjust, but regular movement often reduces the need for over-the-counter laxatives.

14.5 Activity for Women with Sensitive Stomachs

Some women have sensitive digestion or conditions like IBS (Irritable Bowel Syndrome). Overly intense exercise might trigger cramps or sudden bathroom needs. The key is to find gentle or moderate activities that do not shock the system. Examples include:

- **Low-Impact Cardio**: Such as swimming or using an elliptical machine, which reduce strain on joints and might be kinder on the stomach.
- **Shorter, Frequent Sessions**: Instead of a single long workout, splitting movement into smaller chunks throughout the day can help.
- **Focus on Breathing**: Proper breathing techniques during exercise can lower stress and keep the body calm, reducing the risk of spasms in the gut.

Listening to your body is vital. If a certain exercise always causes gut problems, it might be best to switch to something else.

14.6 Support for Women During Menstruation or Pregnancy

Hormone swings during the monthly cycle or pregnancy can influence digestion. Physical activity can help, but adjustments may be needed:

1. **Menstrual Cycle**:
   - Some women feel bloated or tired during the first days of the cycle. Gentle walks or stretches can support bowel function without adding fatigue.
   - Later in the cycle, if energy returns, moderate cardio or strength training can keep digestion moving.
2. **Pregnancy**:

- Many pregnant women experience slower digestion due to high progesterone. Light to moderate activities like prenatal yoga or swimming can help reduce constipation.
    - Avoid exercises that cause too much jumping or impact, especially later in pregnancy. The goal is to help the intestines without straining the abdomen.
3. **Postpartum:**
    - After childbirth, the abdominal muscles need time to recover. Gentle walks are usually a good start. Intense exercise might be too hard on the core right away.
    - Over time, stronger pelvic floor exercises can help with bladder control and also support digestion by stabilizing the abdominal region.

14.7 Stress, Cortisol, and the Gut

Physical activity helps reduce cortisol, the stress hormone that can harm the gut if levels stay high. When cortisol is consistently elevated, it can lead to changes in gut bacteria, slow repair of the gut lining, and even increase the risk of developing sensitivities. By lowering cortisol, exercise helps keep the gut environment more stable.

1. **Natural Mood Boost**: Endorphins released during exercise can offset the negative effects of cortisol, promoting a feeling of calm afterward.
2. **Better Gut Lining**: Reduced stress may support faster repair of gut cells, which is key for preventing leakage of unwanted particles into the bloodstream.

14.8 Tips to Start and Sustain an Exercise Habit

1. **Set Realistic Goals**:
   If you are new to exercise, starting with a daily 10-minute walk might be more manageable than aiming for 60-minute runs right away. This helps build confidence and consistency.

2. **Incorporate Fun Activities**:
   Women who find exercise boring might try dance workouts, nature hikes, or group classes with friends. Enjoyable movement is easier to maintain in the long run.
3. **Use Everyday Opportunities**:
   Instead of always driving, walk short distances. Take the stairs rather than the elevator. These mini-workouts can add up to significant benefits for digestion.
4. **Stay Hydrated**:
   Thirst can be mistaken for hunger, and dehydration can lead to constipation. Sip water before, during, and after exercise.
5. **Listen to the Body**:
   If you feel sharp pains or severe cramping in the gut while exercising, slow down or pause. Pain can be a sign that something is off, like a lack of proper warm-up or an unsettled stomach.

14.9 Combining Exercise with Other Gut-Friendly Habits

Exercise alone can do a lot, but pairing it with other healthy choices can multiply the benefits. Women often get the best results when they view physical activity as part of a bigger plan:

1. **Fiber Focus**:
   Eating enough fiber from whole grains, vegetables, and fruits helps keep the colon active. Combined with exercise, it can reduce the risk of constipation and bloating.
2. **Probiotic Support**:
   Fermented foods or probiotic supplements can help maintain a balanced microbiome. A balanced microbiome plus regular activity sets the stage for a smoother digestion process.
3. **Stress Reduction**:
   Activities like meditation, simple breathing practices, or mild stretching before bed can work alongside exercise to keep stress hormones low.
4. **Regular Meal Times**:
   Staying consistent with meal times allows the body to predict when

it needs to release digestive enzymes. If you add exercise around these times, be mindful of the best pre- and post-meal windows.

14.10 Overcoming Roadblocks

Many women want to be more active but face obstacles:

1. **Busy Schedules**:
    - If you only have small pockets of free time, break workouts into short segments. Two or three 10-minute sessions a day can still provide benefits.
    - Consider moving your body while doing other tasks, such as marching in place while on a phone call.
2. **Lack of Energy**:
    - Fatigue can be common, especially for women with demanding jobs or family duties. Starting the day with a short routine can spark energy for the rest of the day.
    - Focus on foods that give steady energy, like whole grains and lean proteins, rather than sugary snacks that cause an energy crash.
3. **Physical Discomfort**:
    - Joint pain or a previous injury might require gentle exercises like swimming or biking.
    - If you have a sensitive stomach, try exercising at times you know your gut is calm, such as mid-morning or late afternoon, rather than right after a heavy meal.
4. **Embarrassment or Social Pressure**:
    - Some women feel uncomfortable exercising in public. Home workouts with online videos, or walking in less crowded areas, can offer a private setting.
    - Ask a friend to join for support if you prefer company.

Putting It All Together

Physical activity has a remarkable effect on digestion. Even simple habits, such as a daily walk, help the bowels move, lower stress, and might boost the types of bacteria in the gut that support good health. Women can tailor their exercise routine to match their stage of life, personal energy levels, and any ongoing health concerns.

Consistency matters more than perfection. Trying to exercise too hard or too often, especially if you are not used to it, can backfire and cause stress on the body. A moderate, steady approach often leads to fewer digestive problems, better nutrient absorption, and improved overall comfort.

Those dealing with stubborn issues like constipation or bloating may see progress by adding short, regular movement sessions into the day. Strengthening the abdominal muscles can help posture and reduce pressure on the stomach, which might lower reflux or heartburn in some cases. And because exercise generally supports mental wellbeing, it can break the cycle of stress that harms the gut.

For many women, the path forward might be a mix of mild cardio, strength building, and relaxing stretching. The goal is not to push the body to extremes, but to keep it active enough that digestion flows more easily. With time, the gut often becomes more efficient, and the related improvements in energy and mood can encourage an ongoing commitment to physical activity.

By keeping these points in mind and adapting them to personal needs, women can harness the power of physical movement to support better digestive health. This can also lead to stronger immunity, steadier energy, and a sense of wellbeing that goes beyond just the gut. When exercise becomes a regular part of life, many find that their bodies—and especially their digestive systems—thank them with reduced discomfort and improved daily comfort.

Chapter 15

Toxins and Gut Health

Many women try to eat right, stay active, and manage stress. However, there is another piece that can affect digestion and overall wellness: toxins. These are chemicals or substances that can harm the body when too much is taken in. Some toxins come from the environment, while others come from food, water, or household items. Over time, exposure to certain toxins can trouble the gut by upsetting the balance of microbes or irritating the gut lining. This chapter explains the common sources of toxins, how they might affect digestion, and practical tips to lessen daily exposure.

15.1 Where Toxins Come From

1. **Environment**:
    - Air pollution can contain particles like dust, smoke, and chemicals from vehicles or factories. Breathing them may affect the lungs, but some toxins can also reach the gut through mucus drainage or in the water supply.
    - Certain areas might have soil or water contamination from industrial waste or heavy metals (like lead or arsenic). When this enters local produce or drinking water, it can harm the gut.
2. **Household Items**:
    - Cleaning products, paints, or air fresheners often contain chemicals. Some are okay in small doses, but heavy or frequent use can release fumes or residues that may disturb the body.
    - Plastics used for storage or cooking can have substances like BPA or phthalates. These can sometimes leak into food, especially when heated. Such chemicals may affect hormones, which in turn can change gut function.
3. **Personal Care Products**:
    - Makeup, lotions, shampoos, and fragrances may contain chemicals that irritate sensitive people or mimic certain

hormones. Over time, this can upset the body's normal hormone balance, including those that affect digestion.
    - Some deodorants or creams have added metals or chemical fragrances that can trigger rashes or internal stress responses.
4. **Foods and Beverages**:
    - Pesticide residues on fruits and vegetables can be a source of toxins if not washed or peeled.
    - Processed foods often have additives (like artificial colors, flavors, or preservatives) that might bother the gut.
    - Certain fish can contain mercury or other heavy metals if they come from polluted waters.
5. **Water Supply**:
    - Tap water in many regions has chlorine or fluoride added for safety reasons. In correct amounts, these may be fine, but old pipes can leach lead or other metals.
    - Well water may carry pollutants from nearby farms (like fertilizer runoff) or naturally occurring minerals that can become toxic at high levels.

15.2 How Toxins Can Affect the Gut

1. **Microbial Imbalance**:
   The gut has many types of bacteria that help break down food and protect the gut lining. Some toxins may damage these friendly bacteria or encourage harmful strains to grow. This shift might lead to bloating, diarrhea, or other gut troubles.
2. **Gut Lining Irritation**:
   Certain chemicals can irritate or inflame the gut lining, making it easier for unwanted particles to slip into the bloodstream. Over time, this can lead to immune responses that cause discomfort, skin issues, or changes in energy.
3. **Hormone Disruption**:
   Some toxins, called "endocrine disruptors," can mimic or block hormones like estrogen. When hormones shift, it can slow or speed up digestion, change appetite, or alter how nutrients are absorbed.

For women, these changes can be more noticeable during monthly cycles or life stages like pregnancy or menopause.

4. **Liver Stress**:
   The liver cleans out toxins from the blood. If the body faces too many toxins, the liver works harder and might not process nutrients as efficiently. A stressed liver can also affect bile production, which helps digest fats. Poor fat digestion can cause oily stools or discomfort after eating fatty foods.
5. **Long-Term Risk**:
   Repeated exposure to certain toxins might raise the chance of chronic inflammation in the gut, leading to conditions like irritable bowel syndrome (IBS) or other long-term digestive issues. Some toxins have even been linked with higher risk for certain cancers, though many other factors also play a role.

15.3 Women's Specific Vulnerabilities

Women can be more affected by toxins for a few reasons:

- **Hormonal Variation**: Hormones like estrogen and progesterone change throughout life. Endocrine disruptors can magnify these shifts, making the gut more reactive.
- **Body Fat Differences**: Women generally have a higher percentage of body fat than men, and some toxins store in fat tissue. This means women might accumulate certain chemicals over time.
- **Product Use**: On average, women may use more personal care products (makeup, lotions, hair products) that could contain questionable ingredients.
- **Pregnancy and Nursing**: During these times, toxins can pass to the developing child or through breast milk. Protecting the gut and reducing toxin exposure is crucial for both mother and baby.

15.4 Signs That Toxins May Be Hurting Your Digestion

It can be hard to pinpoint toxins as the direct cause of digestive problems, but certain patterns might suggest a link:

- Frequent bloating, gas, or cramps with no clear dietary cause.
- Brain fog or fatigue after using certain cleaning products or being in certain environments.
- Increased skin breakouts, rashes, or hair changes along with gut discomfort.
- Sensitivity to strong smells (like perfume, paint, or synthetic fragrances).
- Headaches, joint pain, or mood shifts paired with digestive upsets that do not improve by simple diet tweaks.

These signs can have many other causes too, so it is important not to jump to conclusions. However, if they persist, looking at possible toxin sources is a reasonable step.

15.5 Reducing Toxins in Your Daily Life

1. **Choose Cleaner Household Products**:
   - Look for brands that list ingredients clearly and avoid harsh chemicals like ammonia or bleach when possible.
   - Use natural solutions like vinegar or baking soda for mild cleaning tasks.
   - Keep rooms well-ventilated when using any cleaning product.
2. **Check Personal Care Labels**:
   - Aim for products without parabens, phthalates, or artificial fragrances.
   - Natural oils (like coconut or jojoba) can replace heavily scented lotions.
   - Choose simple makeup brands that test for heavy metals, especially in lip products.
3. **Improve Air Quality**:

- Open windows to air out rooms if the outside air quality is decent.
- Use an air purifier with a HEPA filter if living in a polluted area or near traffic.
- Avoid spraying air fresheners or scented candles that can add chemicals to the air.

4. **Use Safer Food Storage**:
    - Switch to glass or stainless steel containers instead of plastic, especially for hot foods or liquids.
    - Avoid microwaving in plastic, as heat can release chemicals into food.
    - If using plastic, look for BPA-free labels, but be aware that some BPA replacements might also be questionable.
5. **Wash Produce**:
    - Rinse fruits and vegetables under running water to remove dirt and some pesticides.
    - Peel produce if pesticide exposure is a worry (though you might lose some nutrients in the peel).
    - For those who can afford it, buying organic versions of the most pesticide-heavy crops (like berries or leafy greens) can cut down on exposure.
6. **Mind Your Water Source**:
    - If concerned about tap water, use a filter that can remove chlorine, lead, or other contaminants.
    - Have well water tested regularly, especially if living in agricultural or industrial areas.
    - Keep an eye on local water reports for updates on safety.

15.6 Supporting the Body's Detox Pathways

The body has built-in ways to handle toxins, mainly through the liver, kidneys, and gut. You can support these natural processes:

1. **Liver Health**:
    - Include foods like leafy greens, beets, and artichokes, which some believe can aid liver function.
    - Limit alcohol, which adds stress to the liver.

        - Get enough protein to help the liver produce enzymes that break down chemicals.
2. **Kidney Support**:
        - Drink enough water to keep urine flowing.
        - Avoid too much salt, which can make the kidneys work harder.
3. **Regular Bowel Movements**:
        - Eat fiber to ensure the gut keeps waste moving out.
        - If constipated, toxins can re-enter the bloodstream from the stool.
        - Gentle exercise can help the bowels move more regularly.
4. **Sweating**:
        - Some toxins can leave through sweat. Activities that make you sweat, like moderate exercise, or even time in a warm bath or sauna (if safe for you), might help.
        - Always replace lost fluids by drinking water.
5. **Restful Sleep**:
        - The body does a lot of repair work during sleep.
        - Good rest can support the immune system and help organs function at their best, including those involved in detox.

15.7 Toxins and the Brain-Gut Link

Certain toxins do not just affect the gut but can also reach the nervous system. When the brain or nerves are irritated, it can change how signals move between the brain and the gut, possibly leading to:

- Increased bowel sensitivity (leading to IBS-like symptoms).
- Lower production of helpful neurotransmitters in the gut (leading to changes in mood or stress handling).
- Heightened stress responses that keep the gut inflamed.

Women who notice more worry, trouble focusing, or mood changes alongside digestive shifts might consider whether environmental toxins are playing a part.

15.8 Practical Steps for Busy Women

1. **Small Swaps**:
   - Replace one common household cleaner with a gentler option each month.
   - Try natural deodorants if skin is often irritated.
   - Buy a glass water bottle instead of reusing plastic ones that can break down over time.
2. **Meal Planning**:
   - Plan meals around fresh, whole foods. The fewer packaged foods you rely on, the less exposure you might get from additives or chemical-laden packaging.
   - Soak beans and grains to remove natural substances that can hinder nutrient absorption.
   - If funds allow, buy a few organic items on the "dirty dozen" list or from local farmers who minimize pesticides.
3. **Observe and Test**:
   - If you suspect something at home is causing trouble, consider removing it for a short time. For example, try not using a certain scented product for a week and see if you feel any change.
   - Seek professional testing if you suspect high exposure (like living near an industrial site). Some labs can measure metals, BPA, or pesticides in blood or urine.
4. **Community Choices**:
   - If possible, be involved in local decisions on water quality or pesticide use. Sometimes local groups push for cleaner parks or safer farming methods, which can benefit everyone's health.
   - Share tips with friends or family. Many people do not realize how daily items might contribute to internal stress on the body.

15.9 Myths About Toxin Exposure

1. **Myth**: If it is on the shelf, it must be harmless.
   Fact: Many chemicals are allowed on the market with limited

long-term safety data. While small amounts might be deemed "safe," repeated or combined exposures could add up.
2. **Myth**: You must do an extreme cleanse to remove toxins.
   Fact: The body already has detox systems (liver, kidneys, gut). Focus on giving them support rather than taking risky or extreme products that claim to cleanse.
3. **Myth**: Natural always means safe.
   Fact: Some natural substances can still cause harm if used incorrectly. Arsenic is natural yet poisonous, so it is important to be informed and cautious, whether natural or synthetic.

15.10 When to Seek Professional Help

Minor changes at home can go a long way. But if you have serious concerns or persistent problems like:

- Ongoing digestive issues (bloody stool, severe pain, weight loss).
- High suspicion of heavy metal poisoning (unusual neurological signs, major fatigue, or known contaminated water).
- Unrelenting rashes, headaches, or mood swings that do not respond to simpler changes.

It may be time to see a doctor or specialist. They can test for specific toxins, recommend steps, or refer you to experts who handle complex cases of exposure.

15.11 Balanced Outlook

It is impossible to avoid all toxins. The modern world contains a variety of chemicals. Trying to remove every possible source could lead to overwhelming stress, which is also harmful to the gut. The key is finding a middle path:

- Identify the most likely or high-level sources of harm.
- Make practical changes to lower exposure, like using cleaner products and eating fewer processed items.

- Support the body's natural cleansing processes with a varied diet, good hydration, and enough rest.
- Keep an eye on local news or studies about toxins in your region.

Women who take these steps often notice improved digestion and more stable energy. Many also feel better emotionally knowing they have reduced some environmental strains on their body.

15.12 Steps to Protect Children in the Household

If you have kids, you might worry about their toxin exposure as well:

- **Child-Safe Cleaning**: Using fewer harsh chemicals means fewer fumes for them to inhale.
- **Encourage Handwashing**: Kids tend to put their hands in their mouths. Washing hands before meals can help remove pesticide residues or cleaning product traces they might have touched.
- **Choosing Toys**: Look for BPA-free labels if you buy plastic toys. Avoid older painted toys that could contain lead-based paint.
- **Teach Simple Habits**: Show them how to rinse fruits or vegetables. Explain why it is not safe to drink from old water hoses or random streams.

15.13 Realistic Expectations

Not all digestive issues come down to toxins. Diet, stress, hormones, and genetics all play roles. However, cutting down on harmful chemicals can remove one piece of the puzzle, giving the gut a better chance to stay balanced. For some women, this might reduce unexplained bloating or help with hormone-related digestion issues. For others, it might boost general energy and clarity.

It is also worth noting that improvement can be gradual. If you switch to safer household items, eat more whole foods, and filter your water, it might take weeks or months to see changes. The body needs time to clear out stored substances and repair tissues. Sticking with it can pay off in the long run.

15.14 Final Notes on Toxin Awareness

- **Moderation**: Extremes are rarely the answer. Aim for safer choices where possible without feeling panicked.
- **Stay Informed**: New research about toxins appears often. Following reputable sources (health agencies, scientific journals) can help you make informed decisions.
- **Listen to Your Body**: If you feel better when avoiding certain products or foods, that is a clue. Everyone reacts differently to chemical exposures.
- **Build Community**: Sharing tips with friends or family can lower costs. For example, you can split a bulk order of safer cleaning supplies or produce.

15.15 Conclusion to Chapter 15

Toxins may not be the first thing on a woman's mind when she thinks about gut problems. Yet, over time, exposure to harmful substances can quietly disrupt gut bacteria, inflame the gut lining, and mess with hormones that affect digestion. By learning where toxins come from and taking small, steady steps to reduce them, women can lessen the strain on the body.

Better air flow at home, choosing gentler personal care items, and eating more whole foods are some ways to start. Supporting the liver, kidneys, and gut through healthy routines (fiber, water, rest) helps the body handle what remains. You do not need to become extreme to see benefits. Gradual improvements often bring welcome relief from ongoing digestive annoyances.

The next chapter explores women's health issues tied to digestion. From reproductive concerns to autoimmune problems, we will see how gut health can play a part in many conditions. Understanding these links can guide more targeted approaches to feel better both inside and out.

Chapter 16

Women's Health Issues Linked to Digestion

Women's health is a broad topic that covers hormones, reproduction, mental wellbeing, and more. Digestion can influence many of these areas. There are certain health issues specific to women—or that happen more often in women—that have links to gut health. By exploring these connections, women can find better ways to manage or prevent certain problems. This chapter takes a close look at conditions like endometriosis, polycystic ovary syndrome (PCOS), autoimmune disorders, and more, focusing on how the gut might play a part.

16.1 Endometriosis and Digestion

What is Endometriosis?
Endometriosis is a condition where tissue similar to the uterine lining grows outside the uterus. It can attach to the ovaries, fallopian tubes, or even parts of the digestive tract. This tissue can lead to pain, cramps, or scar formation.

Connection to Digestion:

- Many women with endometriosis report bloating, constipation, or diarrhea around their cycle. This could be due to tissue growth near the intestines or general inflammation.
- Gut inflammation can worsen the pain, and painful cramps can slow or disrupt bowel movements.
- Some research suggests that an imbalance in gut bacteria might increase inflammation, which could add to endometriosis symptoms.

Management Ideas:

- Foods high in antioxidants (like berries or leafy greens) might help reduce overall inflammation.

- Avoiding high-sugar or highly processed items can help keep blood sugar stable and limit added inflammation.
- Light exercises or gentle stretching may ease pelvic tension, possibly helping the bowels move.
- Speaking with a specialist can confirm the diagnosis and suggest hormone treatments or surgery if needed.

16.2 Polycystic Ovary Syndrome (PCOS) and the Gut

What is PCOS?
PCOS is a hormonal disorder common among women of reproductive age. It involves irregular periods or no periods at all, and often high levels of androgens (male hormones). Many women with PCOS also have insulin resistance, making the body less responsive to insulin.

Gut Health Link:

- Insulin resistance can affect how gut microbes function. High insulin may encourage the growth of certain bacteria linked to weight gain or inflammation.
- Some women with PCOS notice more bloating or shifts in bowel habits during hormone fluctuations.
- A gut microbiome lacking diversity might worsen insulin resistance, creating a loop where hormones and digestion feed off each other negatively.

Ways to Help:

- A balanced diet with enough fiber, protein, and healthy fats can support stable blood sugar.
- Exercise, even just walking, often improves insulin sensitivity, which can also help the gut.
- Certain supplements, like inositol or probiotics, might help some women, though advice from a healthcare provider is best.
- Stress management is important because high cortisol from stress can worsen hormone imbalance and harm gut bacteria.

16.3 Autoimmune Disorders and the Gut

Autoimmune conditions occur when the immune system mistakenly attacks the body's own tissues. Women have higher rates of many autoimmune issues, such as lupus, rheumatoid arthritis, and Hashimoto's thyroiditis.

Gut Factor:

- A leaky or inflamed gut might allow tiny particles into the bloodstream, triggering an immune reaction. In some women, this might lead to flare-ups of autoimmune symptoms.
- Certain bacteria in the gut may either protect against autoimmune reactions or make them worse, depending on the balance.

Examples:

1. **Hashimoto's Thyroiditis**:
    - Involves the thyroid gland. Many women with thyroid problems notice changes in bowel habits: constipation if thyroid function slows, diarrhea if it speeds up.
    - Supporting gut health with fiber and probiotics may help keep the immune system calmer, though it is not a cure.
2. **Rheumatoid Arthritis**:
    - Affects the joints, but inflammation can spread through the body. Some women note more joint pain when digestion is off or when certain gut-related infections occur.
    - Lowering gut inflammation with a varied diet might reduce flares.

Lifestyle Tips:

- Identify and avoid foods that spark symptoms. An elimination diet, done with care, can reveal triggers.
- Adequate vitamin D and omega-3 fats may help regulate immune function.
- Gentle exercise and stress reduction can protect the gut and reduce overall inflammation.

16.4 Urinary Tract Infections (UTIs) and the Gut

Though a UTI affects the urinary system, the balance of bacteria in the gut and in the genital area can influence infection risk. Many UTIs occur when harmful bacteria migrate from the bowel. Women have a shorter urethra than men, making it easier for bacteria to enter.

Gut Connection:

- If the gut is dominated by harmful bacteria, they can spread more easily. This raises the chance of UTIs.
- Antibiotic treatment for UTIs can disrupt gut bacteria, possibly causing diarrhea or yeast overgrowth.

Supportive Measures:

- Staying hydrated helps flush bacteria from the urinary tract.
- Eating probiotic foods (like yogurt) or taking specific strains that target urinary health may lower the risk of recurring UTIs.
- Wiping front to back after using the bathroom can reduce the spread of bowel bacteria.
- Avoiding sugary drinks might help, since high sugar can feed harmful microbes in both the gut and urinary system.

16.5 Menstrual Irregularities and Gut Health

Menstrual cycles can vary for many reasons, including weight changes, stress, or hormone disorders. The gut can also play a quiet role in how regular a woman's cycle is. For instance, certain gut bacteria help process estrogen. If these bacteria are too few or overwhelmed by harmful strains, the breakdown of excess estrogen may not happen properly.

Possible Effects:

- Higher estrogen might lead to symptoms like water retention or heavier cycles.
- If the gut is inflamed, the body might pump out stress hormones, which can disturb normal hormone rhythms.

Suggestions:

- Focus on fiber (from oats, vegetables, fruits) to encourage excretion of extra hormones.
- Keep gut inflammation down by limiting overly processed snacks and sugary drinks.
- Note if certain times of your cycle bring digestive changes. Paying attention to these patterns can help you adapt meals or activities.

16.6 Fertility and the Gut

Fertility can be affected by many factors: age, hormone levels, stress, and more. Some experts are looking at whether a healthy gut might also help:

- **Hormone Regulation**: A balanced microbiome may support better hormone balance, which is important for ovulation.
- **Nutrient Absorption**: The gut helps absorb vitamins and minerals needed for healthy eggs, such as folate or iron.
- **Inflammation Control**: High inflammation can disrupt reproductive processes. Maintaining a calmer gut might aid a stable environment for conception.

Women trying to become pregnant might consider boosting gut health by eating whole foods, limiting toxins, and staying active. While it is not a sole answer for fertility, it could be one piece of a broader plan.

16.7 Gestational Diabetes

Some women develop diabetes during pregnancy, known as gestational diabetes. This condition can affect both mother and baby if not managed. Gut bacteria are thought to play a part in how the body handles glucose:

- Studies suggest that mothers with certain microbiome imbalances might have a higher chance of developing gestational diabetes.

- Eating a varied, fiber-rich diet before and during pregnancy can help keep blood sugar stable.
- Healthcare providers might check blood sugar levels more often if there are risk factors (like a family history or being overweight).

16.8 Breastfeeding and Gut Health

Breastfeeding can shape the mother's and baby's gut health:

- The mother's body needs more nutrients, and if the gut is struggling, she might feel extra fatigued or face constipation.
- The baby's first gut bacteria come partly from the mother. A balanced maternal microbiome can pass on more helpful microbes through breast milk.
- Some mothers notice that if they eat certain foods (like spicy dishes or cow's milk products), the baby shows signs of fussiness or gas. This does not happen for everyone, but paying attention can be useful.

16.9 Menopause and Beyond

In older women, hormone levels change and menstruation stops. The gut can be involved in:

- **Bone Health**: The gut needs to absorb calcium and vitamin D well to keep bones strong. As estrogen drops, bone density can go down. A healthy gut may help slow this process.
- **Weight Changes**: Many women gain weight around the abdomen during menopause. The gut microbiome can influence how the body stores fat.
- **Mood and Sleep**: Fluctuating hormones can lead to night sweats or insomnia, which then affect digestion. Calmer gut function might help reduce some discomfort.

16.10 Stress, Anxiety, and Women's Health

Women may juggle many tasks and responsibilities, leading to chronic stress or anxiety. Stress hormones can disturb both the gut and the reproductive system. For example:

- A stressed gut might become more permeable ("leaky"), raising inflammation.
- Chronic tension can alter hormone signals that control ovulation or the menstrual cycle.
- Some conditions like IBS may worsen during times of strong emotional stress.

Strategies for coping with stress—like moderate exercise, talking with a counselor, or practicing breathing exercises—can help keep both the gut and hormones more stable.

16.11 Pelvic Floor and Digestion

The pelvic floor muscles support the bladder, uterus, and rectum. If these muscles weaken or tighten too much, women might have:

- Bladder leaks when sneezing or exercising.
- Trouble passing stool or the feeling of incomplete bowel movements.
- Pain during intercourse or pelvic exams.

Working with a pelvic floor therapist can help. By learning how to properly contract and relax these muscles, some women see better results in bowel regularity and reduced pressure on the abdominal region.

16.12 Dietary Patterns to Help Women's Health Issues

It is impossible to give one diet plan for all women, but some patterns show benefits:

1. **Mediterranean-Style Eating**:
   - Focuses on vegetables, fruits, whole grains, legumes, fish, and olive oil.
   - Rich in fiber, healthy fats, and antioxidants that can lower inflammation.
   - Could support balanced hormones and a varied microbiome.
2. **Balanced Plate**:
   - Half the plate as vegetables, a quarter as protein (beans, fish, poultry, lean meat), and a quarter as a wholesome starch (brown rice or sweet potato).
   - Helps manage portion control and includes key nutrients for hormone and gut function.
3. **Low-GI Foods**:
   - Choosing foods that do not spike blood sugar quickly (like oats, legumes, apples) can stabilize insulin.
   - Helpful for PCOS, prediabetes, or women wanting to keep energy steady.
4. **Avoid Extreme Approaches**:
   - Very low-carb or very high-protein diets may help some women temporarily, but can upset gut bacteria if fiber is lacking.
   - Balance is usually safer long-term unless there is a specific medical reason.

16.13 Supplements and Supportive Tools

While food is the best source of nutrients, certain supplements might aid women with digestive-related health issues:

- **Probiotics**: Specific strains may help IBS, yeast infections, or urinary issues.
- **Omega-3**: Fish oil or algae-based supplements can reduce inflammation, which may ease joint or gut discomfort.

- **Vitamin D**: Low levels of vitamin D are common, especially in less sunny regions. Adequate vitamin D helps with immune function and bone health.
- **Magnesium**: May relieve constipation or muscle cramps, including those related to menstrual cycles.

Before adding supplements, it is wise to talk with a healthcare provider. Over-supplementing can lead to imbalances or side effects.

16.14 When to Visit a Specialist

If you face ongoing discomfort, irregular cycles, or suspect conditions like endometriosis, PCOS, or an autoimmune disease, it may be time to see a doctor who focuses on women's health. They can do thorough checks, such as:

- Blood tests for hormones, inflammation markers, or nutrient levels.
- Imaging like ultrasounds to check reproductive organs.
- Possible endoscopy or colonoscopy if digestive symptoms are severe and unexplained.

Early diagnosis and treatment can prevent issues from getting worse. Gut health might be one factor, but addressing it can help you heal faster or with less medication.

16.15 Tips for Daily Life

1. **Track Symptoms**:
    - Keep a simple journal noting diet, menstrual cycle details, stress levels, and any digestion or pain issues. Look for patterns over a month or two.
2. **Physical Activity**:
    - Move in ways you enjoy—yoga, walking, dancing. This supports both hormone balance and gut function.
3. **Stay Hydrated**:

- Water aids digestion and helps excrete hormones.
4. **Limit Quick Fixes**:
   - Products that claim instant relief or hormone balance might be untested. Trust evidence-based methods when possible.
5. **Partner with Health Professionals**:
   - A dietitian, gynecologist, or gastroenterologist can offer tailored advice.
   - If stress is high, a counselor or support group can be valuable.

16.16 Real-Life Cases

- **Case 1: Leah, Age 28, IBS and PCOS**
  Leah had irregular periods and cramps. Testing showed PCOS. She also struggled with IBS, noticing flare-ups when stressed or after sugary meals. Her doctor recommended moderate exercise, a higher fiber diet (beans, vegetables), and checking insulin levels. Over months, Leah's cycles became a bit more predictable, and her IBS eased when she lowered processed sugar.
- **Case 2: Maria, Age 35, Endometriosis**
  Maria felt severe pain during her period and had diarrhea each month. An ultrasound found endometriosis. With her doctor, she tried hormone therapy and changed her diet to include more anti-inflammatory foods. Gentle yoga helped reduce pelvic tension. While she still had some pain, it was more manageable, and her digestion improved.
- **Case 3: Carol, Age 50, Perimenopause**
  Carol noticed weight gain around her belly, more frequent constipation, and mood swings. Blood work showed she was entering perimenopause. She started walking daily and added ground flaxseed for extra fiber and healthy fats. After some time, her bowel movements became more regular, and she felt calmer. She also adjusted her bedtime to manage night sweats.

16.17 The Role of Mental Wellbeing

Many women's health concerns overlap with mental health. Pain, hormone imbalance, or constant trips to the bathroom can lead to worry or sadness. Meanwhile, stress can increase gut symptoms. A balanced approach often includes:

- Taking time for hobbies or breaks that calm the mind.
- Practicing simple breathing exercises to lower anxiety, which can help the gut.
- Connecting with friends or a support group if isolation is part of the problem.

Women are often caregivers but might not give themselves the same attention. Tuning in to one's own needs is vital for long-term health, including the gut.

16.18 Moving Forward

No matter the specific issue, focusing on the gut can benefit overall wellbeing. Whether the problem is monthly cramps, an autoimmune flare, or concerns about fertility, improving gut function can remove one stress on the body. This does not always solve everything, but it often makes conditions more manageable.

16.19 Staying Informed

Medical research continues to reveal more about the gut's role in women's health. Staying open to new findings—without jumping at every unproven claim—can help women find better solutions over time. Reading from trusted sources or discussing the latest research with healthcare providers can guide safe choices.

16.20 Conclusion to Chapter 16

Digestive health is not separate from the rest of the body. In women, issues like endometriosis, PCOS, autoimmune conditions, or even UTI risk all have some ties to the gut. By caring for the gut lining, maintaining a balanced microbiome, and managing inflammation, women may see improvements in many areas of health.

It is important to remember that each woman is different. Strategies that help one person might not be as effective for another. Patience and a willingness to adjust habits—like diet, exercise, or stress management—can lead to better results. In the next chapters, we will look at herbs and supplements for support, plus daily habits and long-term care for the gut, giving more tools to handle the health concerns that matter most to women.

Chapter 17

Herbs and Supplements for Support

Many women look for extra ways to help their digestive system beyond simple diet and exercise. Herbs and supplements can sometimes fill these gaps, offering nutrients or plant compounds that may support gut function and overall health. While not a replacement for a balanced diet, they can be a helpful addition, especially when dealing with common problems like bloating, low energy, or stress. In this chapter, we will review various herbs and dietary supplements often used for digestion and other health concerns in women. We will explain how they might work, possible side effects, and tips to choose safe and effective products.

17.1 Why Consider Herbs and Supplements?

1. **Address Nutrient Gaps**
   Even with a diet full of fruits, vegetables, and whole grains, some women might still not reach the recommended levels of certain nutrients. Busy lifestyles, digestive problems, or higher demands during stages like pregnancy can lead to shortfalls. A well-chosen supplement can help fill these gaps.
2. **Target Specific Concerns**
   Some herbs are believed to calm the stomach, ease gas, or help with mild constipation. Others might support healthy bowel movements or help the body handle stress. Supplements may offer more concentrated doses of substances that would be hard to get enough of from food alone.
3. **Support the Body's Systems**
   Various vitamins, minerals, or herbal extracts can aid not just digestion but also hormones, immune defenses, or mental balance. When the gut is supported, other body systems may work better, too.
4. **Caution**
   Always remember that herbs and supplements can have side effects or interact with medications. It is wise to speak to a healthcare

professional before adding any new product to your routine. Some supplements can be harmful in large doses or if used improperly.

17.2 Common Herbs for Digestive Health

1. **Ginger**
    - **Uses**: Known for calming nausea and helping with mild stomach upset. Some women use ginger to ease motion sickness or morning sickness in pregnancy, though they should confirm with a doctor first.
    - **Forms**: Fresh root, dried powder, capsules, teas.
    - **Potential Effects**: May help with bloating, help move food through the intestines, and reduce inflammation in the gut.
    - **Safety**: Generally safe in moderate amounts, though very large doses could thin the blood or irritate the stomach.
2. **Peppermint**
    - **Uses**: The essential oil of peppermint has a cooling effect and can help relax the muscles of the gut. This can reduce cramps, gas, or the feeling of a tight abdomen.
    - **Forms**: Tea, capsules with enteric coating, or essential oil (not to be taken orally in pure form unless under guidance).
    - **Potential Effects**: Often used for IBS-type symptoms. Can ease mild constipation or diarrhea by calming spasms.
    - **Caution**: Peppermint might worsen reflux in some people, because it can relax the lower esophageal sphincter and allow acid to move up.
3. **Chamomile**
    - **Uses**: Frequently consumed as a tea. Chamomile may calm the nervous system and help with mild inflammation in the gut.
    - **Potential Effects**: Some believe it soothes the stomach lining and relieves gas or cramping.
    - **Safety**: Generally safe unless you have a specific allergy to plants in the daisy family.
4. **Fennel**

- **Uses**: Known for its licorice-like flavor. Often used to reduce gas or bloating. In some cultures, people chew fennel seeds after meals.
- **Forms**: Seeds, teas, or extracts.
- **Possible Benefits**: May help relax digestive muscles, reduce flatulence, and support regular bowel movements.
- **Note**: Fennel is usually safe in moderate amounts, but concentrated extracts should be used with care.

5. **Turmeric**
   - **Uses**: A bright yellow spice containing curcumin, which has anti-inflammatory properties.
   - **Forms**: Ground spice, supplements, or teas.
   - **Potential Digestive Support**: May help soothe inflammation in the gut, though large-scale studies are ongoing.
   - **Caution**: High doses can thin the blood or irritate the stomach. Those with gallbladder issues should check with a doctor first.

6. **Slippery Elm**
   - **Uses**: Produces a soothing substance when mixed with water. Some women use it to coat the throat or stomach.
   - **Potential Effects**: May help with mild reflux or an inflamed gut lining by providing a protective barrier.
   - **Safety**: Generally safe in moderate amounts, but can interfere with absorption of certain medications if taken at the same time.

17.3 Popular Supplement Types

1. **Probiotics**
   - **Purpose**: Add beneficial bacteria to the gut. Different strains target different concerns, such as diarrhea, constipation, or immune support.
   - **Forms**: Capsules, powders, certain yogurts, or fermented foods.
   - **Tips**: Look for products that list specific strains (e.g., Lactobacillus rhamnosus GG) and colony-forming units

(CFUs). Store them properly, often in the fridge if recommended.
2. **Prebiotics**
    - **Purpose**: Provide fiber or other compounds that feed good gut bacteria.
    - **Common Types**: Inulin, fructooligosaccharides (FOS), or galactooligosaccharides (GOS).
    - **Benefits**: Enhance the growth of good microbes. May help reduce constipation or support immune function.
    - **Side Effects**: Large amounts can cause gas or bloating, so start low and increase gradually.
3. **Digestive Enzymes**
    - **Purpose**: Help break down proteins, carbohydrates, or fats if the body's own enzyme production is low. Some people with pancreatic issues or certain digestive conditions find these useful.
    - **Forms**: Over-the-counter tablets or prescription strength.
    - **Note**: If you do not have a specific enzyme deficiency, you might not see much benefit. Misuse can lead to altered gut function over time.
4. **Fiber Supplements**
    - **Purpose**: Increase dietary fiber intake to help with regular bowel movements and feed beneficial bacteria.
    - **Examples**: Psyllium husk, methylcellulose.
    - **Benefits**: Can relieve constipation, support healthy cholesterol levels, and stabilize blood sugar.
    - **Caution**: Must be taken with enough water to avoid blockages in the intestines. Start slowly to avoid too much gas.
5. **Vitamins and Minerals**
    - **Types**: Women might be low in vitamin D, iron, calcium, or magnesium. Each plays a part in digestion and overall function.
    - **Iron**: Helps transport oxygen in the blood, but can cause constipation or dark stools.
    - **Calcium**: Important for bones and muscle function in the gut.
    - **Magnesium**: Helps with muscle relaxation, including the intestines.

- **Vitamin D**: Affects immunity and potentially gut barrier function.
- **Advice**: Get tested if you suspect a deficiency. Overuse of vitamins can create imbalances or toxicity.

17.4 Specific Concerns and Possible Herb/Supplement Approaches

1. **Stress-Related Gut Upset**
   - **Herbs to Consider**: Chamomile, lemon balm, or lavender in tea form might calm nervous tension.
   - **Supplements**: Magnesium (for muscle relaxation) or certain probiotic strains linked to mood support (like Bifidobacterium longum).
2. **Menstrual Cramps and Bloating**
   - **Herbs**: Ginger and turmeric can help reduce inflammation and ease cramps. Fennel can help reduce bloating.
   - **Minerals**: Calcium and magnesium can sometimes reduce muscle cramps.
3. **Hot Flashes or Menopause Discomfort**
   - **Herbs**: Some women use black cohosh or red clover for menopausal symptoms, although research results vary. If these help ease stress or hot flashes, the gut may also feel more stable.
   - **Caution**: Always confirm safety, especially if you have a history of hormone-sensitive conditions.
4. **Constipation**
   - **Herbs**: Senna is a strong herbal laxative but should be used only short-term. Gentler options might include dandelion root tea (mild diuretic and supportive for the liver) or licorice root (though not for everyone).
   - **Fiber Supplements**: Psyllium husk often helps add bulk to stools.
   - **Hydration**: Essential when increasing fiber or using herbal laxatives.
5. **Reflux or Heartburn**

- **Herbs**: Slippery elm or marshmallow root can coat the esophagus.
- **Digestive Enzymes**: In some cases, low stomach acid can cause reflux, so checking with a professional is key.
- **Probiotics**: Might help if the reflux is partly due to bacterial imbalance.

17.5 Quality and Safety Considerations

1. **Regulation Limits**
   In many countries, herbs and supplements are not as strictly regulated as medications. This means product quality can differ. Some may not contain the listed ingredients, or they could have contaminants.
2. **Reputable Brands**
   Look for seals like "USP Verified" (in the United States) or other third-party testing. Check reviews or talk to a pharmacist for brand suggestions.
3. **Interactions**
   Certain herbs can interact with prescription drugs. For example, St. John's Wort can reduce the effectiveness of birth control pills or antidepressants. Licorice root (especially the form with glycyrrhizin) can raise blood pressure or lower potassium.
4. **Allergies**
   If you have plant or pollen allergies, be cautious with herbal teas or extracts that might trigger a reaction.
5. **Pregnancy and Breastfeeding**
   Many herbs have not been tested thoroughly in pregnant or nursing women. Always double-check safety or speak to a healthcare provider before using supplements in these stages of life.

17.6 How to Choose the Right Supplements

1. **Identify Your Goals**
   Are you dealing with constipation, mild reflux, or stress-related bloating? Pick herbs or nutrients that match your main issue.
2. **Research and Professional Input**
   Read trusted resources. If you have a chronic condition or take medications, ask a doctor or a qualified nutritionist for advice.
3. **Start One at a Time**
   It is wise to try just one new supplement or herb at first. That way, if side effects happen, you will know the cause.
4. **Monitor Effects**
   Keep a small log of how you feel. If you do not see improvement or notice unwanted effects, you might stop or switch approaches.
5. **Stick to the Recommended Dose**
   More is not always better. High doses of some supplements can lead to toxicity or harm. Follow directions on the label or from a healthcare provider.

17.7 Special Supplements for Women's Stages

1. **During Pregnancy**
   - **Prenatal Vitamins**: Contain folate, iron, calcium, and other nutrients for fetal development.
   - **Probiotics**: Some moms find them useful for constipation or to prevent certain infections, but check with your obstetric provider.
   - **Ginger**: Commonly used for morning sickness, but large amounts need caution.
2. **Postpartum**
   - **Iron**: If there was significant blood loss, iron might be needed.
   - **Calcium and Vitamin D**: If breastfeeding, these support both mother and baby.
   - **B-Complex Vitamins**: Help with energy and stress management.
3. **Perimenopause and Menopause**

- **Vitamin D and Calcium**: Important for bone health as estrogen levels drop.
- **Phytoestrogens** (like soy isoflavones): Some women find them helpful, but results vary.
- **Herbs for Hot Flashes**: Black cohosh is popular, though evidence is mixed.

4. **Later Years**
    - **Fiber Supplements**: Constipation can become more common with age.
    - **Joint Support**: Omega-3 fatty acids or turmeric might ease mild joint pain, indirectly aiding mobility for better digestion.
    - **Multivitamins**: Can help fill nutritional gaps if appetite changes or if certain foods become harder to digest.

17.8 Avoiding Over-Supplementation

Some women start piling on products in hopes of feeling better fast—this can backfire. Too many supplements might:

- Overload the liver or kidneys.
- Interfere with each other or with medications.
- Cause new digestive troubles, like diarrhea or cramping.

A balanced approach is best. If you suspect multiple deficiencies, it is often better to get tested so that you know exactly what needs supplementing. Blind guessing can waste money and cause confusion.

17.9 Dietary Methods as First Steps

Before relying on pills and extracts, it is good to make sure basic habits are in place:

- **Eating Variety**: A wide range of colorful foods can offer many vitamins, minerals, and plant compounds naturally.

- **Regular Meals**: Allows the digestive system to work in a predictable pattern.
- **Hydration**: Water helps move nutrients and waste.
- **Enough Protein**: Important for tissue repair and hormone production.
- **Healthy Fats**: Help absorb fat-soluble vitamins (A, D, E, K) and may reduce inflammation.

If these basics are missing, herbs and supplements alone might not give the results you want.

17.10 Combining Herbs and Supplements with Other Care

1. **Physical Activity**
   - Exercise helps blood circulation, ensuring that nutrients and herbal compounds reach body cells.
   - Some herbs might enhance workout recovery if they have anti-inflammatory effects.
2. **Stress Reduction**
   - Chronic stress can neutralize the benefits of certain herbs. For instance, if you take chamomile but still have nonstop stress, your system might remain tense.
   - Adopting relaxation methods can make supplements work better.
3. **Proper Sleep**
   - Sleep is crucial for hormone balance and gut repair. Some teas (like chamomile or passionflower) can promote calmness before bed.
4. **Professional Therapy**
   - For serious gut issues, medical treatments or therapies may be needed. Herbs and supplements can complement, but not replace, professional care in conditions like severe IBS, inflammatory bowel disease, or advanced thyroid problems.

17.11 Examples of How Supplements Help Different Women

- **Case: Alicia (Age 25)**
  Alicia has mild IBS, mostly with bloating and cramps after meals. She starts taking a peppermint oil capsule with an enteric coating before lunch. She also drinks ginger tea when feeling nauseous. Over a few weeks, she notices less bloating. She still pays attention to stress management and meal timing.
- **Case: Brenda (Age 38)**
  Brenda often feels stressed, leading to constipation and tension headaches. She adds magnesium citrate (in a moderate dose) at night to relax muscles and help with regular stools. She also starts chamomile tea in the evening to wind down. This combination, plus short walks during breaks, improves her bowel habits and reduces headaches.
- **Case: Eva (Age 52)**
  Eva experiences hot flashes and mild reflux. She tries a probiotic supplement for her gut and occasionally uses slippery elm to soothe her esophagus. She also looks into black cohosh for hot flashes. Her reflux improves slightly, but she still needs to avoid large meals late at night. Over time, the probiotic helps her bowel regularity, too.

17.12 Myth vs. Reality

- **Myth**: "Herbal means totally safe."
  Reality: Some plants have strong effects, can be toxic at high doses, or may conflict with other medications.
- **Myth**: "I can see results right away."
  Reality: Herbs and supplements often take days or weeks to show effects. Be patient and consistent with use.
- **Myth**: "All probiotic strains are the same."
  Reality: Different strains help different conditions. One strain may ease diarrhea, while another targets constipation or mood support.

17.13 Conclusion to Chapter 17

Herbs and supplements offer extra tools for women aiming to support their gut health. Ginger, peppermint, chamomile, fennel, and turmeric are some popular herbs for easing mild stomach upset or reducing bloating. Supplements like probiotics, prebiotics, enzymes, and certain vitamins or minerals can also help fill nutrient gaps or address specific problems like constipation, mild reflux, or stress-related digestion issues.

Still, caution is vital. Interactions, side effects, and poor product quality can lead to unwanted outcomes. It is best to approach herbs and supplements as part of a well-rounded plan that includes a good diet, regular activity, stress relief, and enough sleep. With wise choices and professional advice when needed, many women find that carefully selected herbs and supplements can improve gut comfort and enhance overall wellbeing.

Chapter 18

Building Good Daily Habits

Eating well and taking occasional supplements can help, but daily habits have a huge effect on the gut. Whether a woman is single, married, a mother, or retired, her routine impacts digestion each day. Simple actions like how fast she eats, the timing of meals, the quality of her sleep, and even how she manages time can shape whether she feels bloated or at ease. This chapter highlights practical ways to form a pattern of living that takes care of the gut.

18.1 Why Routines Matter

Our bodies like consistency. The gut has a biological clock that expects certain patterns in eating, sleeping, and activity. When life is unpredictable, the gut can become confused. This might lead to irregular bowel movements, cravings for sweets, or spikes in stress hormones that damage gut bacteria. By building good daily habits, women give the gut a friendly environment in which to do its work.

18.2 Morning Habits to Start the Day

1. **Wake Up and Hydrate**
    - After hours of sleep, the body is low on fluids. Drinking a glass of water soon after waking helps the digestive tract prepare for breakfast.
    - Warm water with a squeeze of lemon (if tolerated) can give a mild kick to the gut, helping to stimulate a bowel movement.
2. **Regular Bowel Time**
    - Some women find that setting aside a few minutes each morning to use the bathroom trains the body to stay

regular. Rushing out the door may cause constipation if you ignore the urge to go.
    - Relax and give yourself enough time. Stress can tighten pelvic muscles and make it harder to pass stool.
3. **Balanced Breakfast**
    - Including protein (eggs, beans, yogurt) along with complex carbs (oats, whole-grain toast) gives slow-release energy.
    - A small portion of fruit or vegetables adds vitamins and fiber.
    - Avoid gulping down breakfast. Eating too fast can cause bloating or indigestion.
4. **Gentle Movement**
    - A quick walk or light stretches can get blood flowing to the digestive organs.
    - Some women enjoy simple yoga poses in the morning, like "cat-camel" or seated twists, which can gently massage the abdomen.

18.3 Meal Timing Throughout the Day

1. **Avoid Skipping Meals**
    - Skipping meals can lead to low blood sugar, irritability, and then overeating later. The gut may struggle with a sudden large meal after fasting all day.
    - Having consistent meal times trains the body to release digestive enzymes on schedule.
2. **Smart Snacking**
    - If you get hungry between meals, choose snacks with fiber and a bit of protein, like an apple with peanut butter or carrot sticks with hummus.
    - Avoid high-sugar or fried snacks, which can lead to an energy crash or gas.
3. **Eat Calmly**
    - Sit down and reduce distractions if possible. Chew food thoroughly. Digestion starts in the mouth with saliva enzymes, so gulping down food can overwhelm the stomach.

- Rushing meals can also cause you to swallow air, adding to bloating.
4. **Moderate Lunch and Dinner**
    - Giant meals can strain the gut, especially if eaten close to bedtime. Spreading calories more evenly over breakfast, lunch, and dinner helps.
    - If dinner is late, keep it lighter and focus on easier-to-digest foods like soups, steamed vegetables, or fish.

18.4 Handling Busy Days

1. **Meal Prep**
    - Cooking in bulk on weekends can provide healthy options during the week. For example, a large pot of soup or cooked beans can be used in multiple meals.
    - Pre-wash and chop vegetables to save time on busy nights.
    - Store meals in portion-sized containers for quick reheating.
2. **Pack Snacks or Lunches**
    - If you are out for work or errands, having homemade snacks or lunches prevents grabbing random fast food.
    - Keep water or a refillable bottle on hand. Dehydration often triggers cravings or low energy.
3. **Set Alarms or Reminders**
    - If you get so busy that you forget to drink water or eat on schedule, use phone reminders.
    - A quick stretch or a few sips of water every hour can keep the gut from stalling.
4. **Plan for Emergencies**
    - Keep simple items like nuts, seeds, or high-fiber bars in your bag or car. They come in handy if traffic or meetings delay normal eating times.
    - Instant oatmeal packets or low-sugar granola bars can be lifesavers in unexpected situations.

18.5 Managing Stress Moments

1. **Micro-Breaks**
   - During a work shift or a day full of errands, pause for one minute to take slow, deep breaths. This lowers stress chemicals that can disrupt digestion.
   - Some women find guided breathing apps helpful for short breaks.
2. **Mindful Tasks**
   - Instead of hurriedly doing chores, slow down a bit. Focus on what you are doing. This calm approach can reduce the strain on your nervous system, keeping the gut more at ease.
   - If you drink tea, pay attention to the warmth and flavor rather than scrolling on your phone. Let the moment relax you.
3. **Physical Release**
   - If stress builds up, a short walk or gentle stretches can release muscle tension.
   - Tight abdominal muscles can hinder digestion, so relaxing them helps the flow of food through the intestines.
4. **Positive Distractions**
   - During tough emotional days, some women watch a light-hearted show, call a friend, or read a comforting book for a few minutes. This break can reset stress responses that harm the gut.

18.6 Evening Routines for Better Digestion

1. **Avoid Late Heavy Meals**
   - Eating a big dinner right before bed can lead to reflux or poor sleep. If possible, finish your last meal at least 2-3 hours before bedtime.
   - If you need a small snack later, go for something light like a piece of fruit, yogurt, or a handful of nuts.
2. **Wind-Down Activities**

- Switch off bright lights or devices an hour before bed. Screen light can disrupt the hormone (melatonin) that signals sleep.
- Calm activities, like reading a paper book or doing gentle yoga stretches, can reduce tension in the gut.

3. **Temperature and Comfort**
   - A cooler bedroom supports better sleep. Good sleep helps the gut repair and manage hormone levels.
   - Make sure your mattress and pillows support a healthy posture. Lying flat with a mildly elevated head might ease mild reflux.
4. **Limit Alcohol**
   - Alcohol can irritate the stomach and disrupt sleep cycles. If you drink, keep it moderate and avoid doing so close to bedtime.
   - Over time, alcohol can shift gut bacteria and increase the risk of inflammation.

18.7 Key Parts of a Consistent Routine

1. **Meal Patterns**:
   - Aim to eat at roughly the same times each day. This helps the gut anticipate meal times and release digestive juices on schedule.
2. **Sleep Schedule**:
   - Going to bed and waking up at consistent times supports circadian rhythms, influencing gut motility and hormone release.
3. **Regular Movement**:
   - It does not have to be high-intensity. Even 20-30 minutes of walking or light exercise most days can keep the bowels active.
   - Sitting too much can slow digestion and increase bloating.
4. **Stress Check-Ins**:
   - Notice when you are clenching your jaw or tensing your shoulders. Loosen up and take a deep breath. This small effort can make digestion smoother.

18.8 Habit Stacking and Motivation

1. **Tie New Habits to Existing Ones**
   - If you already brew coffee in the morning, take that moment to drink a glass of water.
   - If you do a 10-minute clean-up after dinner, add a short walk around the block before or after.
   - Linking new behavior to a routine you do automatically makes it easier to keep going.
2. **Set Realistic Goals**
   - Start small. If you never eat breakfast, try having a piece of fruit and a boiled egg first. Gradually build up.
   - Overly ambitious goals can cause frustration and lead to quitting.
3. **Track Progress**
   - A simple checklist or calendar where you mark days you followed a habit can keep you motivated. Seeing a string of successes builds momentum.
4. **Reward Yourself Wisely**
   - Instead of a sugary treat, pick a non-food reward: a favorite show, a relaxing bath, or new socks for your walks.
   - Positive reinforcement helps turn a behavior into a regular pattern.

18.9 Overcoming Common Barriers

1. **Lack of Time**
   - Try to combine tasks: While cooking dinner, prepare extra servings for tomorrow's lunch.
   - Use weekends or a less busy weekday evening for meal prep.
   - Keep exercise short but consistent. Even 10 minutes of movement is better than none.
2. **Cravings and Snack Attacks**

- Sometimes cravings come from thirst or boredom. Drink water first. If you are still hungry, pick a filling snack with fiber and protein.
- Plan snacks. Having a container of chopped veggies or fruit ready can stop you from reaching for candy.

3. **Social Pressures**
   - Friends or family might offer sugary desserts or encourage skipping meals. Politely say you are focusing on your digestion and appreciate their support.
   - Share your reasons if you feel comfortable. Sometimes people back off when they understand you have a clear health goal.
4. **Stressful Life Events**
   - During major life changes (new job, moving house, illness in the family), habits can slip.
   - Aim to keep at least one or two core habits: drinking water and having breakfast, for example. Once life settles, return to the full routine.

18.10 Monitoring Your Gut's Response

1. **Symptom Journal**
   - Write down any episodes of bloating, constipation, or reflux, plus what you ate, your stress level, and your sleep hours.
   - Over time, you might see patterns: for instance, late-night meals lead to morning reflux, or skipping lunch triggers overeating at dinner.
2. **Energy Levels**
   - Note how you feel after certain meals or at different times of day. Do new habits help you have steadier energy?
   - Feeling sluggish after lunch might mean you need a lighter meal or a short walk afterward.
3. **Bowel Movements**
   - Healthy bowel movements differ from person to person, but a general goal is 1-2 comfortable, complete movements per day.

- Watch for changes in color, consistency, or frequency. Big shifts might signal the need to adjust diet or see a professional.
4. **Mood Tracking**
    - Mood can show how well your gut is functioning. If you are more irritable or anxious, the gut might be under stress.
    - Notice if feeling edgy lines up with missed meals, poor sleep, or too much sugar.

18.11 Practical Tools

1. **Kitchen Tools**
    - A slow cooker or pressure cooker can help prepare beans, stews, or soups. This saves time and yields healthy meals.
    - Good storage containers make meal prep easier, and you can freeze extras for busy days.
2. **Apps**
    - Nutrition apps can log meals and show macronutrient intake, though do not become obsessed with numbers.
    - Water reminder apps can ping you to sip liquids regularly.
    - Simple note apps let you track mood, digestion, or to-do lists.
3. **Support Systems**
    - A spouse, friend, or coworker can join you in building healthy habits. Accountability helps.
    - Online communities or local groups focused on healthy cooking or mild exercise can keep you inspired.

18.12 Habit Changes for Different Life Stages

1. **Young Adults**
    - Schedules might be irregular with school or early career demands. Setting meal times and carrying healthy snacks can reduce fast food reliance.
    - Building strong habits now sets a good base for later.

2. **Mothers of Young Children**
   - Meal planning and batch cooking can ease the chaos.
   - Incorporating children in simple cooking tasks can teach them about healthy eating and keep your routine on track.
3. **Midlife Stress**
   - Work, caregiving for older parents, or teen children can push healthy habits aside.
   - Make self-care a priority at least in small doses—like a 15-minute daily walk or a weekly meal prep session.
4. **Seniors**
   - Metabolism changes, and mobility might decrease. Keep moving with low-impact exercises to help digestion.
   - Adjust meal sizes if appetite shifts, focusing on nutrient-rich foods to maintain muscle and gut health.

18.13 Combining Habits with Professional Guidance

If digestive troubles persist despite good habits, it may be time to seek help:

- **Medical Checkups**: Rule out conditions like thyroid problems, gallbladder issues, or more serious gut diseases.
- **Dietitians**: Can customize a plan if you have allergies, intolerances, or special needs (e.g., pregnancy, diabetes).
- **Therapists**: If stress or emotional eating is the root, counseling can assist.

Professionals bring outside knowledge that might pinpoint blind spots in your daily routine or diet.

18.14 Fine-Tuning with Time

Habits are not rigid rules. They should adjust as life changes:

- **Changing Seasons**: In colder months, you might prefer more soups and warm teas. In summer, lighter, fresh meals might suit your gut better.
- **Illness or Injury**: Sometimes recovery calls for different food textures or more rest.
- **Personal Growth**: You might learn new recipes or find new physical activities you love. Update habits so they continue to serve your needs.

18.15 Real-Life Examples

- **Laura's Lunch Routine**: Laura realized she skipped lunch while working from home. This led to overeating at dinner and nighttime heartburn. She started preparing lunch the night before, putting it in a visible container in the fridge. She also set a calendar reminder at noon. Over weeks, her reflux lessened, and she felt more energetic in the afternoon.
- **Dana's Nighttime Unwinding**: Dana used to watch TV in bed with bright lights, and she often munched on chips. She woke up bloated. She decided to end screen time an hour before bed, switching to reading a light novel in dimmer lighting. She replaced chips with a cup of herbal tea if she felt like snacking. Soon, she woke with less bloating and slept better.
- **Fiona's Family Meal Prep**: Fiona had two kids and a full-time job. She shopped on Saturdays and batch-cooked on Sundays, making large pans of roasted veggies, chicken, and brown rice. She stored them in containers for easy lunches and dinners. This cut down on fast food. Her kids also learned about balanced meals, and her digestion improved as she ate more fiber and fewer takeouts.

18.16 Small Wins and Steady Progress

It is easy to expect huge results fast, but the gut responds best to consistent, gentle care. Making one or two changes at a time and sticking with them can be more powerful than drastic overhauls that do not last.

Celebrate small victories: a week of regular bowel movements, a drop in bloating, or fewer sugar cravings. Such successes build momentum for the next step.

18.17 Avoiding Perfectionism

Life events, holidays, or travel can disrupt routines. Aim for balance rather than strict perfection. A few days off track will not ruin everything, as long as you return to healthy habits. Guilt and stress can be just as harmful to the gut as junk food. Give yourself room to adjust and learn.

18.18 Teaching Others

As you find routines that work, you might share them with friends or family. You do not need to lecture or pressure them, but you can offer tips if they ask. This creates a supportive environment where everyone can encourage each other's healthy choices. Children, in particular, learn by watching. If they see you take care of your digestion, they might do the same as they grow.

18.19 Looking Ahead

Building daily habits is an ongoing project. As you see benefits—like improved energy, better mood, or fewer digestive problems—you will likely feel motivated to keep going. In the next chapters, we will explore long-term care for the gut and look at examples and stories from women who have made big improvements by taking these steps. Remember, small efforts over time can lead to meaningful change. By managing stress, eating balanced meals, and honoring your body's need for consistent rest, you help your gut operate at its best, today and tomorrow.

18.20 Conclusion to Chapter 18

Good daily habits are the foundation for a healthy gut. While single changes—such as adding fiber or a probiotic—may help, a strong routine amplifies those benefits. Starting the day with water, eating meals on a schedule, moving your body, and winding down before bed all provide structure that supports smooth digestion. Even when life throws curveballs, holding onto key habits can keep the gut from tipping into discomfort.

By setting realistic goals, tracking progress, and staying flexible, women can gradually shape a lifestyle that nourishes the digestive system. In turn, they may see improvements in energy, mood, weight stability, and overall wellness. The gut thrives on consistency, and each day's actions matter. With practice and patience, these daily habits become second nature—a core part of how you care for yourself.

Chapter 19

Long-Term Care for the Digestive System

The gut is a complex system that changes over time. It does not stay the same from childhood to old age. Some of these changes come from aging, while others happen because of our daily habits, medical conditions, or life events. Knowing how to care for your gut in the long run can bring stability and comfort. In this chapter, we will look at long-term strategies for protecting your digestive health. We will talk about how to plan for different phases of life, watch out for shifting needs, and deal with problems that might show up.

19.1 Why Think Ahead?

Many people pay attention to the gut only when something goes wrong, like a bad case of heartburn or a sudden stomach upset. But the best way to avoid big problems is to have a plan. That plan can include regular check-ins with a doctor, small changes in your daily habits, and ways to handle new conditions if they arise. By thinking long term, you can prevent many troubles. You can also notice early signs that your gut needs extra support.

Benefits of Long-Term Planning:

- Fewer surprises if you already know your body's patterns
- Less worry because you have tools to handle changes
- More consistent energy and comfort from day to day
- Better mood and clearer thinking when the gut is calm

19.2 The Role of Regular Check-Ups

Some women see their doctor or healthcare provider only when they feel very ill. A better approach is to go for routine exams at a reasonable interval (often once a year, though it can vary). During these visits, you can ask questions about digestion, mention any small changes you have noticed, and possibly catch early signs of a problem before it grows.

What to Discuss:

- Bowel habits: Are they regular? Have they changed?
- Eating patterns: Do certain foods now cause discomfort that used to be fine?
- Stress levels: Are you dealing with chronic tension that might harm the gut?
- Family history: Some gut diseases may have a genetic component, so share that info if you have it.

It is also wise to get recommended screenings when you reach certain ages. For instance, many healthcare systems suggest a colonoscopy starting at a certain age to check for colon polyps or cancer. If you have a family history of these conditions, your doctor may want you to start screenings earlier.

19.3 Watching for Signals That Something Changed

The body is not static. Even if you build good habits, your gut can shift due to hormonal changes, new medications, or lifestyle differences (like moving or changing your job). Paying attention to small signs can prevent bigger issues later.

Possible Signals:

- A sudden change in stool frequency (fewer or more bowel movements)
- Bloating or cramps at times that used to be fine
- Ongoing heartburn or acid reflux, especially if it becomes more frequent
- Unexplained tiredness that does not go away with rest
- Changes in appetite, such as never feeling full or never feeling hungry

Not every sign points to a serious health issue. Still, it is good to note these changes in a simple journal. If they persist, you can share the notes with your healthcare provider.

19.4 Adjusting to Life Stages

Different life stages bring different gut needs. Below are some common stages and tips for each:

1. **Young Adulthood (20s to Early 30s)**
   - Rapid lifestyle changes can include moving away from home, building a career, and possibly starting a family.
   - Schedules might be hectic, leading to less focus on meal timing or balanced diets.
   - Building strong gut habits at this stage—like a fiber-rich diet, moderate exercise, and regular meals—can pay off later.
2. **Midlife (Late 30s to 40s and 50s)**
   - Some women find that hormone changes start to appear. Digestion can slow, or new sensitivities might arise.
   - Work and family duties can be heavy, raising stress. Stress management can be key to preventing gut discomfort.
   - Planning healthy snacks and smaller, balanced meals can help with stable energy levels and bowel regularity.
3. **Menopause and Beyond**
   - As estrogen and other hormones shift, the gut microbiome might change. Constipation or bloating could become more common.
   - Nutrient needs can shift. For instance, you might need more calcium or vitamin D to support bones, which also links to muscle function in the gut.
   - Physical activity that suits your fitness level can keep digestion moving and support muscle tone.
4. **Older Adulthood**
   - Appetite might go down, or chewing could be harder. Adjusting food textures and focusing on nutrient density becomes more important.

- Hydration and regular movement remain essential to avoid constipation.
- Keeping an eye on medication side effects is important, as seniors often take multiple prescriptions that can affect gut function.

19.5 Preparing for Possible Setbacks

Even with good plans, setbacks can occur. You might catch a nasty gut bug, develop new food sensitivities, or go through a stressful event that weakens your immune system. Knowing how to bounce back is vital.

Practical Steps:

- Have a "comfort plan": easy-to-digest foods (like soups, rice, bananas) ready in the pantry if you get sick.
- Keep hydration solutions or simple electrolyte drinks on hand for times when diarrhea or vomiting strikes.
- If you take antibiotics, remember to speak to your doctor about possibly using a probiotic afterward to rebuild healthy gut bacteria.
- Adjust your schedule for rest if stress becomes high. Taking short breaks or lowering non-essential tasks can give your body space to heal.

19.6 The Value of Periodic Dietary Tweaks

The gut can get used to the same foods day after day. While stability is good, adding variety can introduce new nutrients and feed different strains of beneficial bacteria. Sometimes, a small tweak can help break a plateau and bring back balance.

Ideas for Dietary Tweaks:

- **Try a new grain**: Instead of only eating white rice, experiment with quinoa, barley, or bulgur.

- **Vary produce**: Each week, pick a new vegetable or fruit that you do not usually buy.
- **Use different spices**: Herbs and spices like cumin, basil, or rosemary can add antioxidants and fresh flavors.
- **Review protein sources**: If you always eat chicken, try fish or beans for a change.

Also, watch out for changes in your tolerance to certain foods. If dairy starts causing issues, you might switch to lactose-free versions or try calcium-fortified plant-based drinks. If you notice wheat leads to bloating, you might test out alternative grains in a careful way, though it is best to confirm with a professional to rule out celiac disease before making big changes.

19.7 Physical Activity and Body Maintenance Over Time

As you age, your muscle mass tends to decline unless you do something about it. Muscles play a role in the gut, too. The intestines rely on smooth muscle to move waste through. Also, your core muscles help keep good posture, reducing pressure on the stomach.

Long-Term Movement Suggestions:

- Strength training with light weights or resistance bands to keep muscles from shrinking.
- Activities like tai chi, yoga, or swimming for gentle, low-impact fitness.
- Short, brisk walks multiple times a week if intense exercise is not your preference.
- Stretching routines to maintain flexibility, preventing cramps or stiffness that can slow digestion.

19.8 Managing Stress as Life Shifts

Long-term gut health also involves emotional health. Big events like job changes, retirement, illness in the family, or changes in living arrangements can raise stress. High levels of stress hormones can upset the gut barrier, leading to more inflammation and less helpful bacteria.

Ways to Manage Long-Term Stress:

- Plan daily or weekly breaks for yourself, even if just 10 minutes of calm.
- Keep a hobby that relaxes you, such as gentle crafting, gardening, or listening to music.
- Learn and practice breathing techniques to quickly lower heart rate and tension.
- Seek support when needed. Talking to a counselor, friend, or support group can help avoid internalizing stress.

19.9 Paying Attention to Medication Side Effects

Over a lifetime, women might be prescribed various medications for blood pressure, thyroid problems, arthritis, or other conditions. Some drugs affect the stomach or intestines directly. Others might change hormone balance, leading to gut shifts. Keeping track of medication side effects can save you from long-term damage.

What to Do:

- Ask your doctor about possible digestive side effects before starting a new medication.
- If a prescription upsets your stomach, note how and when it happens. You may be able to switch drugs or adjust the dose.
- Use protective strategies. For example, some medicines should be taken with meals to avoid irritation.

19.10 Setting Goals for the Future

Some women like to plan health goals each year. This could be part of a personal routine, like at the start of a new year or on a birthday. Setting gut health goals can keep you motivated. For instance:

- **Goal**: Increase daily fiber intake by adding one new high-fiber food each week.
- **Goal**: Drink at least 6-8 cups of water a day if you currently drink less.
- **Goal**: Walk for 30 minutes, 5 days a week, to keep the bowels active.
- **Goal**: Try a new recipe with a vegetable you rarely eat once a month.

These little targets can remind you to stay on track. By checking them off, you see your progress, which can encourage you to keep going.

19.11 Handling Mild Chronic Conditions

Some digestive conditions become mild but long-term, like low-level acid reflux or an ongoing sensitivity to certain foods. You do not have to let these conditions rule your life if you have a plan to manage them.

Ideas:

- For low-level reflux, avoid heavy meals before bed. Elevate your head slightly while sleeping. Chew food well and eat slowly to reduce swallowing air.
- For mild lactose intolerance, try lactose-free milk or small portions of dairy with meals.
- For IBS that flares with stress, adopt a relaxation routine or talk with a therapist who specializes in gut-focused therapy.

19.12 Staying Flexible Over the Years

One main point of long-term care is flexibility. The strategies that worked in your 20s might need changes in your 40s, 60s, or beyond. Rather than seeing this as a failure, view it as an expected part of aging. The body's needs shift, so it makes sense that your gut health methods change, too.

Keys to Flexibility:

- Notice new signals. If certain foods cause mild discomfort that did not before, test removing or reducing them to see if it helps.
- If you have a new medical diagnosis, look up how it interacts with gut health.
- Adjust portion sizes if your activity level changes. If you move less, large meals can overload your digestion. If you move more, you may need extra fuel.

19.13 The Influence of Community

Living a healthy life is easier when you have social support. Sharing ideas with friends or family can keep you on track. Sometimes, women feel alone in their gut struggles, but you are not alone. By talking about it in safe environments, you may find others with similar questions or tips.

Ways Community Can Help:

- Cooking clubs or potluck events where healthy dishes are shared
- Local or online groups for gentle fitness activities
- Book clubs that also discuss health topics occasionally
- Family members who also want to improve their eating habits, so you can prepare meals together

19.14 Checking for Advanced Care

If you do everything right—balanced eating, regular exercise, stress management—but still face symptoms like ongoing pain, severe bloating, or weight changes, it might be time to step up care. Some conditions need advanced testing or specialized procedures. For example:

- **Gastroscopy**: To look at the esophagus and stomach lining if you have chronic reflux or pain.
- **Colonoscopy**: For suspicious changes in bowel habits or to check for polyps when you reach a certain age.
- **Ultrasound or CT Scan**: If you suspect gallstones or other organ issues causing belly pain.

Never ignore serious or repeated warning signs. Early detection can help fix a problem or manage it better in the long term.

19.15 Creating a Supportive Environment

It is easier to maintain good gut health if your environment encourages it. That can include your home, workplace, or social circles:

- **Kitchen Setup**: Keep your pantry stocked with staple items for quick healthy meals (beans, lentils, brown rice, herbs).
- **Workplace**: If possible, store healthy snacks in a desk drawer or a small fridge. Take short walks during breaks to reduce stiffness and encourage bowel movement.
- **Social Life**: Suggest potlucks or gatherings where healthy recipes are appreciated. Instead of meeting only at restaurants, maybe plan a walk in the park or an outdoor meet-up.

19.16 Using Technology for Long-Term Support

Tech can help you stay on track:

- **Apps for Meal Planning**: Some apps let you plan healthy meals for a week. This avoids daily guesswork and impulse choices.
- **Step Counters**: Simple trackers on phones or watches can remind you to move if you have been sitting too long.
- **Symptom Trackers**: If you deal with a chronic gut concern, an app that logs symptoms, foods, and stress can spot patterns.
- **Online Groups**: Support forums or social media groups might inspire you with new recipes or routines. Be careful, though, to follow reliable health advice.

19.17 The Reward of Consistency

Small, consistent actions can pay off more than drastic measures. When you keep to a steady routine—moderate exercise, balanced meals, good hydration, and stress management—your body often repays you with a calmer digestive system. This does not mean you will never have an upset stomach or a stressful day, but it reduces the frequency and severity of problems.

Over many months and years, good habits can protect you from bigger issues. They can also make you more in tune with your body, so you catch changes early.

19.18 Teaching Future Generations

If you have children or young people in your life, you can show them by example how to build healthy routines. This can prevent them from facing major gut problems later. Simple things like showing them how to eat vegetables with each meal, how to drink water regularly, or how to handle stress can shape their future.

You do not need to lecture them. Let them see you prepare balanced meals and enjoy them. Invite them to help you cook or pick out fresh produce. These experiences can build a positive view of self-care and gut health.

19.19 Making Peace with the Process

Caring for the gut is not about being perfect. Life events, holidays, or travel might make you eat differently for a while. Accept that you will not always eat the "ideal" meal or keep the "ideal" schedule. The key is returning to your routine once you can. Do not let guilt or shame creep in. The gut is resilient, and it can bounce back with consistent support.

19.20 Conclusion to Chapter 19

Long-term care for the digestive system relies on consistency, awareness, and flexibility. By checking in with your healthcare provider regularly, watching for signals of change, and adjusting your routine as life evolves, you give your gut the best chance to stay strong. Different stages of life need different approaches, but the fundamentals—balanced diet, enough water, moderate exercise, stress control—remain helpful throughout.

Even if small problems come up, having a plan can make the difference between a quick fix and a lingering issue. Over time, these steps also support energy, mood, and overall health. In the final chapter, we will look at examples and stories from women who have navigated a variety of gut-related challenges. Their experiences can show how these ideas play out in real life, giving you practical insights for your own path.

Chapter 20

Examples and Stories

Sometimes, the best way to understand how to manage gut health is to hear from others who have walked that path. In this final chapter, we share stories of women facing different digestive problems or transitions. Each example shows how daily habits, mindset, and a bit of creativity can lead to improvements. While no single story will match your life exactly, you might find ideas or inspiration. The goal is to show that solutions often come from a mix of knowledge, simple actions, and listening to your body.

20.1 Sarah: Balancing Work and Gut

Situation:
Sarah is 29, works a desk job, and lives in a busy city. She started having regular bloating and mild constipation in her mid-twenties. At first, she thought it was just "normal." But the discomfort got worse. She also began feeling overly tired after lunch, as if her body was using all its energy just to digest food.

Key Issues:

- Skipping breakfast to hurry to work
- Grabbing fast meals at her desk, often processed snacks or takeout
- Barely moving during the day, leading to stiffness and slow digestion
- High stress from tight work deadlines

Small Changes, Big Results:

1. **Morning Meal:** Sarah decided to get up 15 minutes earlier to prepare oatmeal with berries. This gave her a more balanced start without rushing.
2. **Hydration:** She kept a 1-liter water bottle on her desk and set a goal to finish it by lunchtime, then refill for the afternoon.

3. **Scheduled Breaks**: Every two hours, she set a silent phone alarm. She used that time to stand, stretch, or take a quick walk to the water cooler.
4. **Lunch Revamp**: Instead of ordering greasy meals, she packed lunches like a salad with beans and nuts or a wrap with grilled chicken and vegetables. If she had to order out, she chose soup and half a sandwich or a small serving of rice with vegetables.
5. **Evening Relaxation**: She practiced a simple breathing exercise for 5 minutes after getting home to lower stress.

Outcome:
Within a few weeks, Sarah noticed she felt less bloated. Her bowel movements became more regular, and the afternoon "slump" was not as severe. She still had stressful days, but her body handled them better. Her main lesson was that small, steady changes in eating and moving can help balance the gut.

20.2 Lisa: Easing Acid Reflux

Situation:
Lisa is 40 and has occasional acid reflux. At first, it only happened after spicy meals or too much coffee. But over time, she began experiencing reflux at least three times a week, even waking up at night with a burning feeling in her chest. She also felt a sour taste in her mouth some mornings.

Key Issues:

- Late-night meals with heavy sauces
- Drinking multiple cups of coffee, especially in the afternoon or after dinner
- Stress about family finances and an aging parent
- Lying flat immediately after eating because she wanted to watch TV on the couch

Steps Taken:

1. **Meal Timing**: Lisa made a rule: no big meals within two hours of bedtime. If she got hungry, she had a small piece of fruit or herbal tea.
2. **Coffee Limit**: She reduced coffee to one cup in the morning. In the afternoon, she switched to herbal tea.
3. **Rest Position**: Instead of lying flat on the couch, she sat upright in a chair after meals or took a gentle walk. For bed, she raised her upper body slightly by propping up the bed frame at the head.
4. **Calmer Evenings**: She found that reading a physical book or doing a light puzzle lowered her evening stress, helping her stomach produce less acid.
5. **Watching Trigger Foods**: She kept a quick list of foods that caused more reflux (like tomato sauce, onions, and deep-fried items). She did not cut them all out forever but limited them or paired them with gentler foods.

Outcome:
Her reflux attacks dropped from three times a week to maybe once a week. Sleep improved because she was not waking up coughing or with a burning chest. The biggest surprise was how much nighttime stress had fueled her reflux. By calming down and adjusting how and when she ate, she found relief without needing daily medication.

20.3 Mona: Dealing With IBS

Situation:
Mona is 35 and has been diagnosed with Irritable Bowel Syndrome (IBS), leaning toward constipation. She gets severe bloating and crampy pain, especially when she is nervous. She also notices that certain foods (like beans or dairy) can worsen her symptoms, but she is not sure which ones are the main culprits.

Key Issues:

- Inconsistent fiber intake—sometimes too much at once, sometimes too little

- High anxiety around mealtimes, worrying if a certain meal will trigger pain
- Poor water intake because she disliked the taste of plain water
- A cycle of skipping meals then overeating out of hunger

Approach:

1. **Food and Symptom Journal**: Mona wrote down what she ate and how she felt for a month. Patterns emerged, such as more bloating on days she had ice cream or beans combined with stressful events.
2. **Gradual Fiber Adjustment**: She added fiber slowly. Instead of a big bowl of bran cereal, she chose a moderate amount of oats or a slice of whole-grain toast. This cut down on gas.
3. **Water Flavoring**: She put slices of cucumber or lemon in water to make it more appealing, aiming for at least 6 cups daily.
4. **Smaller Portions More Often**: Eating in smaller servings throughout the day eased the load on her gut. She had mini meals like half a sandwich, a small salad, or a cup of soup.
5. **Stress Management**: Mona tried short guided meditations to handle anxiety. She also learned that a gentle walk after eating helped reduce cramps.

Outcome:
Her IBS did not vanish overnight, but the daily bloating and cramping calmed down. She found a better balance of fiber and fluids, and her anxiety over mealtimes went down once she identified certain triggers. The consistency of a food journal and stress practice made her feel more in control.

20.4 Dina: Hormone Changes and Constipation

Situation:
Dina is 47 and perimenopausal. Her periods are more spread out, and she feels more tense than before. She started having constipation lasting a few days at a time, making her feel heavy and uncomfortable. She worried that she might need laxatives regularly, which she did not want.

Key Issues:

- Hormonal shifts slowing gut motility
- Skipping workouts because she felt too tired
- Drinking mostly coffee or tea, very little plain water
- Irregular meal times due to her unpredictable schedule

Plan:

1. **Hydration Routine**: Dina set a clear goal to drink a glass of water first thing in the morning and another mid-morning, plus more in the afternoon. She reduced coffee from four cups a day to two.
2. **Fiber-Rich Foods**: She added prunes or dried figs to her breakfast cereal. She also replaced white pasta with whole-wheat versions.
3. **Light Evening Exercise**: On most nights, she took a gentle 15-minute walk after dinner. This physical movement before bedtime helped her sleep better and supported bowel movements the next day.
4. **Better Sleep Habits**: She tried to go to bed at the same time each night, avoiding large meals or stressful phone calls right before bed.
5. **Occasional Mild Supplements**: She used a mild fiber supplement on days when she felt especially blocked, but tried to keep it occasional, relying more on natural foods.

Outcome:
Over a couple of months, Dina's constipation episodes shortened and became less severe. She found that consistent hydration and a short evening walk were key. Although perimenopause still brought some ups and downs, these new habits softened the impact on her gut.

20.5 Karen: Dealing with Multiple Food Sensitivities

Situation:
Karen is 34 and realized that certain foods were leaving her with skin rashes and stomach pain. She suspected lactose was a problem, but she also noticed wheat products sometimes made her feel heavy. After a breath

test, she confirmed lactose intolerance. However, she tested negative for celiac disease. Still, wheat seemed to irritate her stomach.

Challenges:

- She felt overwhelmed avoiding both dairy and too much wheat.
- Grocery shopping became a puzzle as she checked all labels.
- Social events felt awkward because she did not want to burden hosts with special demands.

Strategies:

1. **Professional Guidance**: She met with a dietitian who helped her map out what to remove and what to keep. Together, they tested how much wheat Karen could handle without discomfort.
2. **Meal Prep**: She planned meals that used gluten-free grains like rice, quinoa, and oats labeled "gluten-free." For dairy, she switched to lactose-free milk or almond milk.
3. **Focus on Natural Foods**: Instead of buying many packaged "free-from" products, she based meals on vegetables, fruits, lean proteins, and simple grains. This lowered the risk of hidden irritants.
4. **Social Adaptations**: Karen brought a small dish to gatherings that she knew she could eat, so she would not feel left out or hungry. She also learned to politely communicate her needs in advance.
5. **Tracking Improvements**: She kept notes on her gut comfort and skin condition. This helped confirm that small amounts of wheat once in a while were okay, but large servings daily caused issues.

Outcome:
Karen felt less stressed and more in control once she had a plan. She discovered that complete avoidance of wheat was not necessary, but moderation was key. Lactose-free dairy allowed her to still enjoy cheese or ice cream in limited amounts. She found a balance that fit her body rather than an extreme approach.

20.6 Elena: Recovering from a Family Crisis

Situation:
Elena is 50 and experienced a sudden family emergency. For a few months, she lived in and out of hospitals while caring for a sick relative. During that time, her own digestion took a back seat. She ate fast meals, snacked on vending machine items, and lost sleep.

Gut Effects:

- Frequent diarrhea when under heavy stress or after too much coffee on an empty stomach
- Overall fatigue and mild depression
- No exercise, constant tension in her shoulders and abdomen

Steps to Rebuild:

1. **Accepting Help**: Friends offered to bring homemade meals to the hospital. She learned to say "yes" to these kind gestures, so she had better food options.
2. **Simple Food Choices**: She picked bland, gentle foods like plain rice, bananas, or light soups when her stomach felt raw.
3. **Controlled Coffee**: She cut coffee down to one cup in the morning, switching to herbal tea in the afternoon to calm her nerves.
4. **Mini Rest Sessions**: In the hospital waiting room, she took 5 minutes to close her eyes, breathe slowly, and ease the tension in her shoulders.
5. **Gradual Return to Routine**: Once her relative stabilized, Elena went back to some older healthy habits—like a short walk each evening and a balanced breakfast. She saw a counselor to process the emotional strain, which also helped her gut settle.

Outcome:
Though it took time, her diarrhea episodes dropped. She regained energy as she resumed better eating and light exercise. The key lesson was that big stress can derail gut health quickly, but a return to basic self-care can help rebuild stability.

20.7 Nina: Building Gut Habits with Her Kids

Situation:
Nina is 36, has two children aged 8 and 10. She wants them to grow up with strong digestion and fewer problems than she faced. She herself had IBS in her 20s. Now mostly under control, she wonders how to pass on good habits to her children.

Actions:

1. **Family Meals**: Nina makes an effort to cook at home and eat together at the table. This helps everyone slow down, chew properly, and talk about the day.
2. **Involving Children**: She asks her kids to help rinse vegetables or measure rice. They learn to recognize fresh foods and appreciate them.
3. **Reducing Sugary Snacks**: She replaced sugary cereal with oatmeal and berries. For treats, she sometimes bakes healthier muffins using whole-wheat flour, letting her kids pick the add-ins (nuts, raisins).
4. **Modeling Behavior**: When Nina feels stressed, she tries not to rush or skip meals. She explains to her kids that food is fuel, and water is important.
5. **Movement Together**: They do family walks or bike rides on weekends. This keeps them active and fosters healthy digestion for all.

Outcome:
Her children see healthy eating as normal, rather than a chore. Nina notices she also benefits because she is practicing what she wants them to learn. Her IBS flares are less frequent because she stays consistent.

20.8 Jocelyn: Finding Her Way in Retirement

Situation:
Jocelyn is 65, recently retired. She thought she would have plenty of time to cook and exercise, but found herself napping often and feeling bored. She

started munching on junk food while watching TV. She also noticed that she felt more gassy and had mild constipation.

Changes:

1. **Daily Schedule**: Jocelyn set up a simple daily plan with a wake-up time, a short walk in the morning, meal times, and a bedtime routine. This gave her structure and reduced mindless snacking.
2. **New Hobbies**: She joined a community gardening club, which got her moving and taught her how to grow fresh vegetables. Harvesting her own produce encouraged her to cook healthier meals.
3. **Fiber Focus**: She made sure each day included at least two servings of fruits, two servings of vegetables, and a whole-grain option. She also tried new recipes that used beans or lentils.
4. **Cutting Down on Sodas**: She realized she was drinking multiple diet sodas daily. She reduced this by substituting water with lemon slices or herbal teas.
5. **Gentle Core Exercises**: She found a senior-friendly yoga class that taught easy poses to strengthen abdominal muscles, helping with bowel movements.

Outcome:
Over months, Jocelyn felt more energized. Her gut was happier, and her mild constipation eased. She saw retirement as a chance to build new healthy habits rather than slipping into inactivity.

20.9 Lessons from These Stories

1. **Small Steps Count**: Each woman made modest changes (meal timing, more water, short walks) that added up. There was no single "magic trick."
2. **Know Your Body**: Tracking foods, noticing stress triggers, and trying new approaches helped them learn what worked.
3. **Routines Help**: A basic framework for meals, movement, and rest can keep the gut stable, even in busy or stressful times.

4. **Ask for Aid**: Whether from a professional, friends, or family, support can make a difference when life is hectic.
5. **Be Flexible**: Needs change over time, so it is okay to shift your strategy as you age, face new conditions, or adapt your lifestyle.

20.10 Conclusion to Chapter 20

Real-life experiences show that digestive health is not about perfection. It is about finding routines and habits that fit each stage of life, each personality, and each body's needs. The stories we have shared highlight the power of small, consistent choices. These choices can range from meal prep to mindful breathing, from short walks to adjusting certain foods.

In each case, these women discovered that the gut is responsive. When cared for, it can adapt and improve, even if problems arose from stress or certain foods. The process took time, some trial and error, and a willingness to learn. Yet each person found that their efforts were rewarded with less discomfort and more comfort in daily life.

Final Words:
You now have knowledge about how the gut works, how it connects to hormones and stress, what foods and nutrients matter, how habits shape digestion, and how to plan for the long haul. You have also seen examples of how women overcame different digestive issues through practical steps. These stories and lessons can guide you in building a plan that suits your own lifestyle. Remember, the goal is not perfection or zero problems forever. The goal is a stable foundation so that when challenges come, you have the tools to handle them, recover well, and keep going with a body that feels supported and a mind that feels at ease.

www.ingramcontent.com/pod-product-compliance
Lightning Source LLC
LaVergne TN
LVHW012103070526
838202LV00056B/5607